D1063825

POEMS & TEXTS

POEMS & TEXTS

An Anthology of French Poems, Translations and Interviews with Ponge, Follain, Guillevic, Frénaud, Bonnefoy, Du Bouchet Roche, and Pleynet

Selected and Translated, with Interviews and an Introduction by
SERGE GAVRONSKY

OCTOBER HOUSE INC *New York*

Published by October House Inc
55 West Thirteenth Street, New York

Library of Congress Catalog Card Number LC 68–29818
Printed in the United States of America

Acknowledgments

FRANCIS PONGE: La barque; Éclaircie en hiver; La Gare; Mœurs nuptiales des chiens; Le soleil lu à la radio (sects. 1–10) *from* LE GRAND RECUEIL III © Editions Gallimard, 1961. Déclaration: Condition et destin de l'artiste *from* TEL QUEL, printemps 1968.

JEAN FOLLAIN: L'empailleur d'oiseaux; Les passions *from* EXISTER © Editions Gallimard, 1947. Écouter; La pomme rouge *from* TERRITOIRES © Editions Gallimard, 1953. Instant; Le Feu; Accords; Artisans; Boutique *from* DES HEURES © Editions Gallimard 1960. Époques *from* POÈMES ET PROSES CHOISIS © Editions Gallimard 1961.

GUILLEVIC: Exposé (fragments) I; *poème extrait de* TERRE À BONHEUR © Editions Seghers, 1952. Il tremblait devant la lumière; Souvenir; Ils ont dit oui *from* EXÉCUTOIRE © Editions Gallimard, 1947. Il y aura toujours dans l'automne *from* GAGNER © Editions Gallimard, 1949. L'école publique *from* TRENTE ET UN SONNETS © Editions Gallimard, 1954. Encore une fois; Tu viens et tu vas; Tous les paysages *from* CARNAC © Editions Gallimard, 1961.

ANDRÉ FRÉNAUD: Il n'y a pas de paradis; Les morts sont toujours jeunes; Machine inutile; Espagne; Pays retrouvé; Qui possède quoi? Les Fils bleus du temps *from* IL N'Y A PAS DE PARADIS © Editions Gallimard, 1962. L'Irruption des mots *from* ANDRÉ FRÉNAUD © Editions Seghers, 1963. Haineusement mon amour la poésie *from* POÈMES DE DESSOUS LE PLANCHER © Editions Gallimard, 1949.

YVES BONNEFOY: Poèmes I, II, III, IV, V, VI, VII *from* DU MOUVEMENT ET DE L'IMMOBILITÉ DE DOUVE © Mercure de France 1953. Aube, fille des larmes, rétablis; Une Voix; La même voix, toujours; L'Oiseau des ruines *from* HIER RÉGNANT DÉSERT © Mercure de France 1958.

ANDRÉ DU BOUCHET: L'Air soudain; Relief; Sol de la montagne; Le Glacier; Rudiments; Le Moteur blanc *from* DANS LA CHALEUR VACANTE © Mercure de France 1961.

DENIS ROCHE: Poèmes 1, 2, 3, 4, 5, Monsieur le pilote *from* LES IDÉES CENTÉSIMALES DE MISS ELANIZE © Editions du Seuil, 1964. Elle n'a plus non plus mes fêtes directement; Après avoir ainsi manifestement ma réalité *from* RÉCITS COMPLETS © Editions du Seuil, 1963.

MARCELIN PLEYNET: Un Palais; Sous la vitre *from* PROVISOIRES AMANTS DES NÈGRES © Editions du Seuil, 1962. L'Arbre en prose *from* PAYSAGES EN DEUX SUIVI DE LES LIGNES DE LA PROSE © Editions du Seuil, 1963. Parler; ces matinées; C'est toujours le même mot; Alors si nous nous retournons; Nos paroles ne seront point aveugles; *from* COMME © Editions du Seuil, 1965.

Contents

Preface

The American poet writes poetry. He may then think about its implications and even comment upon these in a philosophic vein. He will often criticize his own works, reading into them, after he has finished them, unexpected themes and ideas.

The French poet, if one is allowed this generalization, is a phenomenon of a different sort. He is first of all a thinker, or at least would wish himself to be one, and consequently takes himself and his philosophy very seriously. Often he has every right to do so. In the tradition of French letters, a tradition that dates back to the Pléiade in the sixteenth century and extends to contemporary works, French poets have first sought to place their writing in a general philosophic and esthetic movement. The rash of manifestos and schools that abound in histories of French literature is a most eloquent testimony to this passion for explication. The French poet finds it almost a spiritual necessity to declare his intentions before writing "creatively."

This difference explains why we in the United States are so unaccustomed to the appearance of a philosophic poet—a redundancy in France. The American poet writes and then keeps quiet. When he does establish himself as a critic it is as a critic that he is considered, and even then, there is a traditional Anglo-Saxon reluctance on his part to immerse himself in metaphysical or philosophical debates. Such debates seem to be peculiarly French. If the reader is not ready to grant this latitude of expression to a French poet, he removes from the poet's intellectual and artistic make-up one of the gifts that so often go to contribute to his merits as a poet. Philosophical pursuits, then, are not eccentric commitments: to the French poet they are the very matter that he exploits artistically.

The poems included in this selection must therefore be taken in two ways. They are poems in the ordinary sense in that they portray as vividly and as concretely as possible a vision of the world in a novel way; they are texts, in that they offer, after the first reading, an example of the philosophic views entertained by the authors themselves. The French poem is intent upon isolating not just the immediate sensation but the concomitant Truth that must find its way to the surface of the written statement.

In asking the reader to embark upon a reading of this volume one is asking, in effect, that he prepare himself for a novel experience. Here he will find much that is both poetic, in the sense that the contemporary French poet understands that word, and significant in its philosophic overtones. The combination should once again testify to the fascinating differences that exist between the French and the American mind.

From Surrealism to Structuralism

Surrealism, until very recently, stood at the heart of the French poetic experience of the twentieth century. That movement, which at first avoided a purely esthetic formulation, succeeded in harnessing the dominant currents evolving from the Symbolists, DADA, and the politically conscious orientation of the thirties.

Surrealism evolved, in turn, into one of the characteristics of Existentialism, that philosophic statement most acceptable to the post-war generation which sought for a means of communicating with a world that had been broken by the war and then officially revived by a return to a political system not too dissimilar from that of the Third Republic.

Those who, adrift after the war, could no longer find accommodation with the Surrealism of André Breton, were absorbed by Existentialism, the new cultural synthesis. The Sartre-Camus Merleau-Ponty group, to which a large number of Parisian intellectuals adhered, declared the supremacy of responsibility, emphasized the moral significance of man's actions, and examined at length —and often in a complex terminology—man's anguish at being forced to decide for himself issues that affect humanity.

"Any man's death diminishes me, because I am involved in Mankind." So wrote John Donne; and now, with infinite care in the deliberate constitution of a vocabulary that would accommodate such an ethical position, the Existentialists proceeded, in literature and philosophy, to explore contemporary problems. Believing, along with Edmund Husserl, in the necessity of carefully describing a phenomenon whenever it appeared, and without recourse to classic epistemology, the movement provided a rallying point for confronting the post-war experience.

The preoccupation with the phenomenon and its objective description led Jean-Paul Sartre to admire the work of Francis Ponge, whose *Le Parti pris des choses*, published in 1942 by Gallimard, described with precision, and in an anti-lyrical style, the most ordinary things. As Husserl had hoped to establish phenomenology as a non-anthropological science, so Ponge, technically, appeared to deal with the phenomenon itself aside from its personal context. This philosophic analysis did not prove fruitful, as Ponge himself admitted, but it did show the possible relationship between Ponge's total accusation of society in his selection of things, and Sartre's equally insistent desire to restructure the human experience—something the Surrealists had forcefully advocated in their period of dominance.

Francis Ponge, already advanced in age, thus benefited from a fortuitous concordance between a systematic philosophical inquiry and his own intellectual position. However, if on the surface Ponge seemed to be mainly preoccupied with things, in reality, not things but language was to prove the underlying principle of his work.

It is indicative of Ponge's position vis-à-vis the avant-garde that if the Existentialists were the first to discover and popularize him, his second, and what he believes is a more incisive reading, occurred with the coming of a new literary generation particularly sensitive to the function of language per se. Francis Ponge has spoken very clearly on this matter and it is consequently an appropriate beginning to the understanding of the major shift in French post-war poetry to investigate briefly what direction Ponge has given to recent literary developments, taking into consideration first his search for a new vocabulary and secondly, his preferred themes.

Ponge readily admits that the language we use has not been accurate in its reflection of the world, since it was perverted by lugubrious and often masochistic preoccupations with ideology that has characterized so much of Western literature. The glorification of man since the Renaissance has adulterated and misdirected the primal power of the word.

In order to recoup this fundamental loss, Ponge had to rediscover language through a careful study of etymology, and primarily through the *Littré* (the dictionary of the history of the French language). He constructed his own vocabulary, one that would most succinctly represent things in their own nature, rather than having them always placed in the perspective of man's biased vision. Taking 'things' as subject matter is thus a conscientious effort to reformulate the moral basis of the world, eliminating the excessive layers of meanings that have warped our view of the material substance of the universe.

Armed with a vocabulary, the next step was to evolve a suitable rhetoric, a means of using this solid, this virtuous language to combat the debilitating lyricism which he considered had destroyed the essential vitality of language.

But in selecting 'things' as the least controversial elements in the world, as the unrecognized structure of our existence, Ponge was not indicating an interest in materialism as an entity in itself. Rather, as he has often maintained in his writings, the object described is both text and pretext. "*Parti pris des choses égale compte tenu des mots*"—or, roughly translated, *things* equal *words*. Ponge suggests that the object being described is actually a vehicle for a linguistic exercise. In *Les Mûres*, for example, he writes:

Aux buissons typographiques constitués par le poème sur une route qui ne mène hors des choses ni à l'esprit, certains fruits sont formés d'une agglomération de sphères qu'une goutte d'encre remplit.

On the typographical shrubs constituted by the poem on a road which leads neither out of things nor to the mind, certain fruits are formed by an agglomeration of spheres that are filled by a drop of ink.

Or again, this time reverting back to one of the sacred cows of French intellectual formulas, Ponge reinterprets Descartes' *Cogito ergo sum* (I think therefore I am). In his study of the seventeenth-century poet, Malherbe, with whom he strongly identifies, Ponge writes:

Pour commencer par la première proposition de ce livre, dont les mots que tu te trouves en train de lire font déjà effectivement partie, voici, me semble-t-il, que j'en ai déjà infligé l'évidence: puisque tu me lis, cher lecteur, donc je suis; puisque tu nous lis (mon livre et moi), cher lecteur, donc nous sommes (Toi, lui, et moi).

Let us begin with the first proposition of this book, of which the words you are now reading are already an effective part. Here it seems to me that I have already inflicted the evidence: since you are reading me, dear reader, therefore I am; since you are reading us (my book and I), dear reader, therefore we are (You, it and I).

Language is thus brilliantly put into the light: it is the substance of the written text before anything else intervenes. All subject matter is secondary. Things that have been chosen have been selected as representational, as allowing language the necessary context in which to express itself.

But language is not an abstraction. It is a social institution: it signifies and connotes. It is rich in historical meanings; it contains, in its etymological evolution, the document of our civilization, so that Ponge does not neglect, cannot neglect, the ultimate need to speak of man. *L'Homme est l'avenir de l'homme* (Man is the future of man), Ponge wrote in his *Notes premières de l'homme.* (Sartre quoted this maxim in his *L'Existentialisme est un humanisme.*) But with this distinction, that while Existentialism reinforced the traditional humanistic bias that had been implanted in Western philosophy, Ponge sought to deal more realistically with the actual position of man in the material world, attributing to him, once again, a considered place, but not an unique one.

Thus, if things, and the necessary rhetorical inflections that he has cultivated, appear to dominate, Ponge indicates that this is meant as a training, as a way station to the proper study of men.

La lessiveuse, le savon, à vrai dire, ne sont encore que de la haute école: c'est l'Homme qui est le but . . .

The washerwoman, soap, to tell the truth, are only steps on the way: the actual goal is Man himself . . .

To treat man objectively, Ponge had to perform a purgatorial operation on the most cherished ideals of Western civilization, insisting that no truth could be reached without first defining the very means, language, that one was about to use. His extraordinary text *Le Savon* consequently takes on a highly moral relevance.

If Ponge has come to consider man in this new perspective, it was not solely due to his linguistic preoccupation. For the greater part of his life, he was active in the Left, only breaking with the Communist party in 1947. In his search for a stable point of reconstruction, no doubt membership in the party came to seem incongruent with his belief in the inauthenticity of so much of our existence in all of its manifestations, including politics. Perhaps his *Malherbe* is indicative of this shift, as it reinforced the elitist view of Ponge the writer, through his hero's insistence on control and the absence of sentimentality.

As he moved away from the polemics of the party, Ponge moved closer to a Mallarméan concept of poetry, a position that seemed to justify his new attitude. No longer searching for the humanistic man, Ponge refuted all attempts at subjecting his inquiry to obsolete definitions, including poetry itself. A Pongian aside expresses this: *La poésie, merde pour ce mot.**

Indeed, if Francis Ponge has focused attention upon himself, it is partially due not only to the undeniable hardness of his prose, its authority, its revelations and its prestigious success in entering the language of the object, but also his damning the old ways of considering not only language but man himself.

Those who have been particularly fascinated by this shift, typified in Ponge's writing, but voiced in other fields as well, have designated the current period, at least the 1960's, as a period of crisis. Some would, with Roland Barthes, consider the new apolitical "abstract" literature as part of a structural reversion. Others consider the literary crisis a reflection of a much wider cultural metamorphosis, preceding yet forcefully influenced by the formation of the Fifth Republic. In any case, as M. Foucault, one of the leading revisionist cultural historians has expressed it, if Marxism was History in the nineteenth century, language has become History today.†

Younger poets and critics such as Marcelin Pleynet, Denis Roche, and Philippe Sollers (author of a *Ponge* in the Seghers series of *Poètes d'aujourd'hui*), have been impressed by the relevance of so much of Ponge's thought to their own efforts at reaching a new definition not only of criticism, but of literature and language itself. Language has become of primary concern, and in their magazine, *Tel quel*, founded in 1960, these three writers, together with others like Jean Thibaudeau (himself author of a study of Ponge), have provided a platform for some of the most systematic, militant, intelligent and irritating criticism of the sacred texts of French literature. They write in their

* Quoted in *Tel quel*, printemps, 1964, Number 17, p. 56.

† *Tel quel*, hiver, 1964, Number 16.

own jargon, involving structural linguistics seasoned with a heavy dose of Freud. They have split themselves off from the Sorbonne treatment of literature and the nineteenth-century socio-historical approach formulated by Sainte-Beuve and Hippolyte Taine.

These young Turks and their admirers have indicated the direction that avant-garde exploration of French letters was to take in the sixties. If one momentarily subsumes all the factions under one banner, that banner would be, as Ponge has explicitly stated, *language* and, as the French understand it, *l'écriture*. And with this they make a concerted plea for the recognition of language as a scientific fact, capable of being analyzed and discussed on the same level as one of the pure sciences.

To understand this preoccupation with linguistics, one has to remember the constant feeling of disadvantage that literary historians have felt vis-à-vis their scientific colleagues. Nostalgia also plays its part—a desire to regain the certainty of a by-gone age where one could discuss, as in the seventeenth century, such things as style, tone, and vocabulary with a large degree of common agreement as to the sense of the words and their connotations. Science has become, since Auguste Comte and Charles Darwin, the objective scale on which all things must be weighed, and it is understandable that in the humanities—and now at last in literature—there has been a powerful movement to appropriate the authority of "pure" science.

One must note another significant development—the work of the pioneers in linguistics in the early decades of the twentieth century. Among these were Roman Jakobson, Troubetzkoy, Hjelmslev, Martinet and Harris, and preeminently Ferdinand de Saussure, who, in his course in general linguistics given at the University of Geneva between 1906 and 1911, succeeded in describing the content of linguistics, enunciating its general principles, plotting out its semiological apparatus, and providing a basic vocabulary to treat synchronic and diachronic linguistics.

Whereas the problem of language was often overlooked by literary critics (and a special praise accorded the transparent style of André Gide, for example), it is now agreed that one cannot disregard the structure of language if one seeks to understand patterns of thought. Syntax becomes the key not only to grammar in its traditional sense but it is also the means that makes accessible the undercurrents of a writer's intentions. This has acted as a corrective to the effusive subjectivity of so much of French poetry and literature. More than ever before, the writer is forced into a state of cognition as he composes. He becomes simultaneously author, narrator, actor, and reader.

Thus, as words gain a new position for themselves, the emphasis moves away from existential and historical considerations to purely linguistic ones. Such is the fervor engendered by the structuralist rage that recently a recondite work appeared introducing mathematical proofs to structural linguistics.*

The written text must now be observed as a reality unto itself, controlled and modeled after rules that are solely applicable to the verbal substance, and determined by structures that are not at the volitional disposal of the individual writer, but that belong, in a wider sense (as Claude Lévi-Strauss has noted) to their own primal development. The analogy to myths is instructive. Much as myths arise out of the plural experience of mankind, little affected by spatial or temporal conditions, so language arises out of an equally communal experience. As Saussure taught, language is a social institution, and there is thus a very close relationship between ethnology and linguistics.

The critic Charles Nisard wrote in 1852†:

C'est de ce nom pompeux que j'ai dû nécessairement intituler le chapitre [*linguistique*] *où il est traité de l'argot . . .*

It is by this pompous word that I have been forced to call this chapter [linguistics] where I have discussed argot.

How increasingly serious and committed the successors of Nisard have become! The Structuralists, whether in the field of psychoanalysis, mathematics, ethnology or linguistics, have become latter-day Knights Templar, holders of the sacred Truth. In crusading for their convictions they have succeeded in dominating a large segment of current French critical writing, as well as French literature itself.

This far more intensive appreciation of language has resulted in a

* Solomon Marcus: *Introduction mathématique à la linguistique structurale*, Paris, Dunod, 1967.

† *Histoire des livres populaires*, Paris, G. P. Maisonneuve et Larose, 1968, II, 355.

reappraisal of the work of the so-called realists among the poets writing in France today, including first of all, the works of Francis Ponge. That is to say, Ponge was first hailed by the Existentialists, who admired what they considered to be his phenomenological treatment of things. But the Existentialist emphasis on historicity, and the importance of man's actions, has been pushed into the background. Much as Jean-Paul Sartre superseded André Breton, so now Claude Lévi-Strauss has edged Sartre off the stage. A parallel exists in the history of the novel and films. In both instances, the label "New" is indicative of a desire to break with the past.

However, from an objective point of view, it is perhaps more instructive to note the manner in which certain key concepts of Surrealism and Existentialism have managed to survive in contemporary thought. (The generally tense intellectual atmosphere that reigns in France may in part be due to doctrinal rigidity and to fragmented schools that follow each other.)

In this carry-over, Freud and his teachings must be given a prominent place. From the time that André Breton became familiar with Freud's theories (Breton indicates 1916 as the date) to Jacques Lacan's recent discussions of Freudian psychoanalytical texts, the influence of Freud has been a constant factor in the exploration of every field of human creativity. Critical differences were often a matter of intensity of interest and degree of familiarity with the Freudian texts, rather than Freudian orthodoxy itself. Freud played an illustrious role in Surrealism. The doctrine of the unconscious defined the basic concepts of that vision of the world. Automatic writing, joint authorship, games of chance, and dream interpretations were all invoked. Breton was certain that a total appreciation of man had been inhibited by overly rationalistic concerns that neglected the larger areas of his existence. Breton was emphatic in his insistence on automatic writing, the heart of his Surrealist theory. He often maintained that without it there would be no Surrealism. Much as Breton admired Freud, however, the Surrealists themselves were not really committed to a systematic study of Freud's writings, very few of which were translated into French. Their "Freudian" interpretations were often based on insufficient knowledge of Freud.

Existentialist psychoanalysis, under the aegis of Jean-Paul Sartre, evolved a more coherent presentation of its fundamental concepts allied to Husserl's phenomenology and to Martin Heidegger's Existentialism and the work of such theoreticians as Adler and Janet, Piaget and Bachelard. Freud was not forgotten, but the role of the unconscious was de-emphasized. Jean-Paul Sartre rejected both the Kantian idealism that pervaded much of European philosophy, and Freud's insistence on the primacy of the unconscious. Phenomenology, the importance of the thing itself, had become an essential part of Sartre's views, and led him to stress what Harry Stack Sullivan called "interpersonal relationships." As a philosopher deeply interested in psychoanalysis, Sartre had nevertheless taken a position contrary to that adopted by the Surrealists. Phenomenological psychoanalysis, as it has been elaborated by Sartre, stresses man's freedom and his capacity to act without being hampered by his unconscious. Is it any wonder, then, that Sartre, attributing a particular grandeur to reason, should have considered the "I" as highly significant, especially when he so dramatically demonstrated the objective absurdity of man's universe!

This substitution of the rational for the irrational could not proceed without calling a counter-movement into being. The pendulum swing of intellectual fashion is such that one might have expected a philosophy based on the rationality of man to provide diminishing returns. In the late fifties, Existentialism was menaced by the rise of Lévi-Strauss's structural ethnology, which was expanded to include "structural" linguistics and much else. Equally impressed with the phenomenological argument, Structuralists reestablished the unconscious as a perfectly viable, and indeed absolutely necessary, concept in dealing with everything from language to cooking and music.

Although the Structuralists do not as yet consider themselves the initiators of a new philosophy, they have all the influence and the prestige of such a school. Structuralists, whether in linguistics, analysis of myths, or their reaffirmation of psychoanalysis, have increasingly sought to reinvest the unconscious with authority and to associate Freud, in a most intimate way, with their critical evaluations. They maintain that much of what we had heretofore assigned to the rational behavior of the individual—our humanistic orientation—

was, in fact, a falsification of the terms of the evolution of the argument. As linguistics has added to our knowledge of comparative grammar, and as ethnologists have revised Lévy-Bruhl's views of primitive man, Sartre's emphasis on human volition, human freedom, and human action now appears to have been an exaggeration of the limits of reality. Structural accounts of these quintessential elaborations, whether esthetic or ritualistic, grant new bases for an assumption dear to the Structuralists—that Hegelian historiographical explanations as well as Sartrean existential doctrines do not conform to observable evidence.

In this simplified version, the Structuralists appear as classicists to the Existentialists' romanticism. The Structuralists believe in the constancy of human phenomena and recognize the role of the unconscious without inflicting upon it either chronological or spatial considerations.

This emergence of the Structuralist methodology parallels another event of the first magnitude: the rise of the Fifth Republic under the authoritarian rule of General Charles de Gaulle. De Gaulle has been an outspoken critic of the party system that led, in his view, to the instability that debilitated the strength and prestige of the French State. After assuming power, and in the ten years prior to the revolutionary outbreaks of the summer of 1968, the Gaullist regime had been particularly successful in turning Frenchmen away from old-style political debates and had reoriented them toward construction of the French economy. He invoked a new sense of national identity, no longer dependent on the immediacy of contemporary history, but, as Bossuet would have envisioned it, in the perspective of History itself.

Until the summer of 1968, the average Frenchman, according to the Gaullist interpretation, was so aware of the need to further the aims of the nation as a whole that the workers, farmers and students—those who had least benefited from his government's domestic policies—would stoically accept the resulting financial restrictions.

And indeed, the Fifth Republic did seem to prove that the Marxist concept of the class struggle, for example, was an outworn principle. Marxism however had not outlived its influence on the French intellectual. On the contrary, it is today as it has been since 1917, an intrinsic part of his philosophic commitment. But Marxism has had to adapt itself to the new currents of thought. Sartre had demonstrated the absence of any necessary division between Existentialism and Marxism, and Louis Althusser, to cite but one left-wing historian, is now trying to accommodate Marxism with Structuralism. (Lévi-Strauss himself, with a Marxist background, is presently working to clarify the relationship between ethnology and Marxism.)

But it is important to realize that classic Marxist economic analysis, heavily steeped in historicism, has been subject to very strong criticism both within and outside the Communist party, and that continued economic prosperity seems to have robbed it of much of its aptness. The conduct of the Communist party during the summer of 1968 demonstrated its loss of revolutionary drive while its condemnation of Russia's invasion of Czechoslovakia has merely underscored the confusion in the party's ideology. The parliamentary elections have borne out de Gaulle's analysis of the French temper. The dedication of a number of students and intellectuals in May, 1968, was insufficient to overcome the fear of a leftist threat to the dreams of those who, increasingly free of political polarization, seek to gain for themselves the material benefits that are usually associated with the United States. Given this sobriety of aim, it is not surprising that a methodology such as the one proferred by the Structuralists should find ready reception among individuals oriented toward a no-nonsense materialist view. The questioning of the political ideologies of the past is thus comparable to that which has been going on in the literary-philosophic domain.

Structuralism, then, is successor to Surrealism and Existentialism, the two preceding fashions of French thought in the twentieth century, while Marxism continues as an essential piety of the intellectual without affecting his rational preoccupations. It is now the custom among French critics and writers to deny the validity of Sartre's theory of commitment and his concept of generosity in literature. With all the emotional involvement of latter-day scholastics, the Structuralists advance their approach to textual criticism, which dispenses with socio-historical references.

The accusation has been leveled at the Structuralists that theirs is not a philosophy. They retort that insofar as "philosophy" like "history" or "literature" has been falsely grounded in historical humanism, it is time to consider an "anti-philosophy," a philosophy without illusions, that will provide an all-encompassing explanation without falling into the fallacy of putting man's ego in the center of the world.

In her work *L'Ere du soupçon* the French novelist and critic Nathalie Sarraute voices the same distrust of traditional assumptions. According to the new criteria she proposes, the writer will no longer think he is capable of emulating the classic nineteenth-century novel where there is an absolute certainty about characters and plot, a certainty that mirrors the stability of the world. Tropisms, those mysterious, sub-verbal means of communication, will become the basic element of psychological analysis. In her latest novel, *Entre la vie et la mort* the emphasis, more than in the previous works, is on writing itself as that which characterizes our activity between life and death.

Thus, freed from ideological positions, from socio-historical determinism as a method of literary criticism, and from classical esthetics, the revolution begun by the structural linguists has provided the necessary ground for an appreciation of the works of those poets included in this volume, men who have been particularly cognizant of the function of language.

The crux of this change is typified by a refusal to accept either the patriotic lyricism of the poets of the Resistance, or the traditional lyricism of French poetry throughout the nineteenth century. Equally strong has been the denunciation of Surrealism's "automatic writing," and loss of interest in the dream—techniques which allowed the poem to proceed free of any interference by the poet acting as a rational being.

Guillevic, Follain, and Frénaud, while rejecting the Surrealists, have retained the traditional preoccupation of the poet, the peculiarly French intensity of concern, for the ultimate question of meaning, truth, and ethical destiny. But for these three poets it is more challenging to come to terms with the reality of the world than to escape from it, and it is more personally courageous to rely on clarity and succinctness than it is to juxtapose flashing images in the hope of happening upon a meaningful poetic statement. It would be impossible for them to produce anything approaching Aragon's *Front*

Rouge, the archetypical political poem, but this does not imply political inactivity or social insensitivity. Both Guillevic and Frénaud have openly dealt with political and social issues, while Follain, Ponge and du Bouchet, in a more veiled manner, have not avoided a political coloration in their poetic works.

As poets these six men have treated different subjects, according to their own temperaments, the times in which they wrote, and the places where they have lived (Ponge, Guillevic, Frénaud, and Bonnefoy are all non-Parisians). But all of them have been fascinated by language, ranging from the poet's traditional preoccupation with the tools of his trade, as in Frénaud's texts, to an outright concentration on language itself, as in Pleynet's works. A critic can appreciate these preoccupations, as well as the influences of Rimbaud, Mallarmé and Lautréamont which still persist. In a letter addressed to Georges Izambard, May 1871, Rimbaud established the distinction between the poet and the person as person: *Je est un autre* (I is another). Frénaud echoes in his interview that he is only infrequently a poet.

Rimbaud's love of childhood themes, however macabre, his social satire, his enthusiasm, his explorations of the boundaries of the imaginary: all these have been significant influences, as well as his admission of failure. On the other hand, *Saison en Enfer* has not been as important to the eight contemporary French poets included in this selection. Neither, it seems to me, have they been willing to spend an Afternoon with a Faun, with the possible exception of Yves Bonnefoy. Nor has the Orphic tradition attracted disciples in this group other than Bonnefoy, and Frénaud in his long mythic poems. If Rimbaud's and Mallarmé's influence have been constant, Lautréamont has become the newly recognized master. "*Ma poésie ne consistera qu'à attaquer, par tous les moyens*..."* Marcelin Pleynet, dedicating his study of Lautréamont to Francis Ponge, shares Lautréamont's intense desire to destroy. In raising Lautréamont to a new critical level, Pleynet also seeks to purify his reputation, so romanticized by the Surrealists.

Mallarmé's esthetics has also been exceedingly influential on each

---

* My poems shall consist of nothing but attack, by any means . . . *Chants de Maldoror*, Chant deuxième.

of the poets, and each has adapted what he specifically needed to perfect his own poems. All have learned from Mallarmé the sanctity of poetry, the special privileges and anguish of writing, the science of writing, the need to form one's own expressive language. Follain, Guillevic and Frénaud are peculiarly indebted to Mallarmé's meticulous attention to language, and to Rimbaud's commitment to the description of daily events.

Jean Follain has been writing steadily and with little change in his style since the early thirties. Volume after volume has appeared imposing Follain's harmonics not by a brutal impact, through a single work, but by the accumulation of a steady number of perfectly welded poems that together contain his convictions and the judgements achieved with growing authority. In prose poems and free verse, Follain has avoided, with the diligence of a judicial mind, the more ecstatic treatments of contemporary problems. There are no religious flights as in the case of Pierre-Jean Jouve or Pierre Emmanuel, nor is there the rhetorical elegance of Saint-John Perse, nor the frivolous touch of Prévert, nor are there any mysterious excursions as projected by Henri Michaux. (And in this, Follain is typical of the other seven poets in this work.)

All that Follain has touched, everything to which he has related, has always borne the distinguishable mark of his own carefully disciplined remembrances. Each poem has a relatively simple architecture that affects the voice, the shape and the content. He has perfected a syntax that plays with unexpected breaks, forcing the doubling back of the lines, as a pivotal end-of-the-line word appears to qualify both what has preceded and what is about to come. This ambiguity, this muted violence which reflects the content, is often accomplished through a gender or a pronoun which allows him to move, imperceptibly, from one level to the next, imposing a high degree of concentration on the reader.

This technical brilliance adds to the value of the poem and helps to define the core of meaning, which is most frequently concerned with the pursuit and rehabilitation of Time. But Follain's salvage of the past is not used as an occasion for emotional distension. Time for him is a perpetual presence, and he succeeds in investing the past with a contemporaneity, devoid of nostalgia. However, in evoking his own past Follain resists the temptation to give it a false historical perspective. The past is summoned to our apprehension untinted by sentimentality. It is rather considered in its temporal evolution: objects are inserted in a temporal context, allowing them to change, metaphorically giving them back their functions now in an absolute condition stripped of an *immense imagerie qui pesait sur les choses* (immense imagery that weighed down on things). He awakens the past to play a new role in the present, and lets the reader perceive through the craftsmanship of the poem itself, as if a veil had been lifted, the very essence of Time momentarily incorporated in the object.

To circumscribe Time, to relate it to its past vitality and to express its present qualities, Follain focuses on everyday utensils, objects that fill our existence and remain anonymous in their formality until the eye and the heart of the poet succeed in drawing attention to them. He seeks, as he says, *embrasser d'un regard des yeux et du cœur ces royaumes fermés* . . . (to seize with a glance of the eye and the heart these closed kingdoms . . .).

His technique is instructive. He systematically removes the excess layers of language, the unjust analogies, the clichés, the myths and the rhetoric that have hidden the objects. Follain, like Ponge, renews not only the sanity of language, but also the prestige of the object. As a lawyer and then as a judge, Follain's professional career has undoubtedly reinforced his cautious disposition toward testimonies and evidence, language and things. But in respecting the authenticity of both, there always arises out of a Follain poem those forgotten kingdoms, an enigmatic presence, different from the one pursued by Bonnefoy, but equally tantalizing. In their exactitude, these poems succeed (as some Surrealist paintings have done) in creating a dual impression—one based on the denotative, and the other on the connotative significances delineated by the word or the object itself. Out of his inexhaustible past, with Rimbaldian insistence, Follain recovers the old tales of violence and maledictions, the debris of reality which he reanimates on the stage of the poem.

Dans les champs
de son enfance éternelle
le poète se promène
qui ne veut rien oublier

In the fields
of his eternal childhood
wanders the poet
who never wants to forget anything

Unlike that of Ponge, the rhetoric is low-keyed and represses a moral stance, acting merely in favor of an inventory of childhood memories without judging them, though often perfuming them with a suggested allegorical touch, a flash of violence, a disturbance, an unknown and charged presence that threatens to destroy the delicate stability that has been established. In this he differs radically from Ponge, who prohibits these "sentimental" allusions, the personal and private recollections of such human emotions as fear, awe or curiosity. Many of Follain's poems, though they evoke the past, do not partake of its gravity: the poem is a trembling thing (that modifier is a frequent one in his poetic vocabulary). It is with the color of blood and an anguished cry that life begins, that the human quality of the poem throbs, that the alliance between the fleeting elements and Time is consummated. The poem is a spectacle, a stage, a niche in Time sequestered in silence where things go back into their past; the end of the poem announces the surprise and the retreat, the evocation and the glance that turns away.

It is as erroneous to apply the label of realist to Guillevic as to Follain, though both have often been so regarded, since both begin, as did Ponge, by accepting the "real" world as the premise of their further observations. But if Ponge and Follain question the validity of language, Guillevic questions the object itself. For him, the exterior world refuses to allow itself to be grasped. It eludes us, it defies us, it exists in a realm that is further away than dead planets. These intransigent objects at which we stare conceal strata of meaning, interior distances, that proliferate as the poet continues to descend into the essence of that which he is defining.

Convinced of the metaphysical nature of objects, Guillevic seeks to go beyond their treacherous façade to the heart of reality. There he will find, unseen except through the poetic definition that embraces them, not only objects, as these are secured in an extremely restrained expression, but also those experiences that are particular to the poet's own life. If there is no doubt about the effectiveness of language as a means of securing the object, there is the perpetual recognition that as the poet approaches the source, it disperses itself, evasive like a mirage. The object is devenomed and left barren of its essential trait. Brevity assures a degree of complicity between the hope expressed in the act of writing and the theme that the poet is anxious to evoke.

Guillevic's style is thus a necessary commitment, allowing a measure of success. The poem, being very short, lasts as long as its effect: it does not exceed the limits of its importance. There is no useless rhetoric, no word lost. The Guillevician cosmos is furnished with Spartan taste, though behind each formula (in the alchemical sense) there lurks a sleeping monster who may wake, as Guillevic reminds us in one of his poems. In other poems he forecasts the day when domesticated animals will revert to their feral ancestry. Like objects, like the poems themselves, animals conceal an energy that is hard to judge and difficult to hear, but transcendent and consequently moving away, evolving outward from an apparently harmless present.

Thus Guillevic attaches himself to the real only to consider it as a transparency, no longer capable of feeding his curiosity. Jean-Pierre Richard in his study of Guillevic points out coats of elusive meanings that are metaphorically rendered in the Guillevician image of an animal being skinned, leaving him as a piece of bleeding meat—part life, part death. In this annulation of life there is a suggestion of common destiny. The same questioning of matter is seen in the image of the tree that begins in complete materiality to finish skyward, taking space in hand, with its sap rising. If such is the nature of objects, Guillevic assumes that the most effective means of attaining them is to turn away from them, involving oneself in the affairs of men, in politics and fraternity. In doing something else, the object reappears unnoticed. (Proust experimented with this technique when he sought to provoke his involuntary memory; Guillevic writes *Les mots c'est pour savoir*—Give me words and I will understand.) Language becomes for Guillevic a mediating force:

Je parle autour de toi
Pour t'épouser quand même
En traversant les mots.

I speak around you
Yet I will marry you
Crossing over words.

A similar nexus exists between words and the object—syntax and vocabulary on the one hand, and substance on the other. But language itself, though its priority is recognized, is ultimately unsatisfactory. It is inadequate because it represents the distance between the object and its transcription. Language proposes an access to that object, which is itself elusive. Silence becomes the mark of suspense, and also of success, when it is conducive to the adhesion of the object with the word. The silence in Guillevic's poems, though not visually represented, introduces an element of fragility in a condition which otherwise is often sensual. Both Bonnefoy and du Bouchet, in different philosophic settings, have espoused this Mallarméan concept of silence which dictates the disposition of their poems on the page as it simultaneously establishes the degree of involvement in the world.

Poetry is Guillevic's way of bringing together interminable fragments, all cut down, and yet all vibrant in their hermeticism. Thus elaborated, they stand momentarily in a lucid light. *Terre de bonheur*, one of his collections, is indicative of his involvement in a world that abounds in chaos, and defies language to reach an accord with the thing that is being described. There is a starkness in Guillevic's world that is reminiscent of his native Morbihan: few colors, few flowers, few edifices. As compensation there is the sea, and this Druidic land—Carnac and its monumental rocks, fearful and reflexive. The starkness of these recollections, found in a well of memories that resembles Follain's, not only mirrors the peculiarities of the Breton coast, but also of Guillevic's own early youth, marked by extreme poverty and stern parental treatment. Does the elusive quality of objects recall in part the inability of the child to convene a stability in his own life? His father, a policeman, was assigned to various posts in France; living in barracks, the family had few opportunities to anchor itself in any one place.

The roots Guillevic did manage to grow seem to have been nurtured by reading German Romantic poets and Lamartine. This may explain the darkness of the landscapes portrayed in Guillevic's poems, and the dual themes that repeat themselves in his works:

aridity, humidity; violence, tenderness (eroticism). Poems cluster around these motifs. They express the militant faith of this member of the Communist party in progress and humanity. And yet, as with Ponge, there has been a disaffection with politics, a decrease in the didactic element in Guillevic's poetry. In constructing his working language, he has freed himself of the esthetics of Surrealism and the ideology of communism. His concern now, as can be seen from his latest book: *Euclidiennes*, is to clarify his universe. Each of these very brief poems assumes, linguistically and metaphorically, the guise of a geometric design. He has gone far from his *Sonnets*, where social commitment was preeminent. The latest poems are oriented toward a Parnassian concept that is devoid of neither humor nor sobriety. Thus the label "realist" that has been imposed on Guillevic is one that has to be interpreted carefully.

André Frénaud's commitment to the world is unquestionable. In contrast to Follain, Guillevic and Ponge, he has not imposed limits on his enthusiasm nor has he delved uniquely into the nature of objects. He ranges over the whole scale of emotions. He does not shrink from granting a proper place to the "soul's impulses" nor to "The highest joy, and the simple pleasure, wonder, nostalgia, bitterness, despair, revolt and rage, goodness . . ." The tone is equally rich as he manages irony, sarcasm, satire, humor and tragedy. Much if not all of his commitment to poetry reverts to a very personal origin. The basis, I believe, is to be found in a very bitter antagonism that he felt toward his parents and that appears in such a line as *Je les mordrai tous mon père et ma mère* (I will bite them both, my father and my mother) and even more explicitly, in that famous line *Je me suis inacceptable . . .* (I am unacceptable to myself . . .), which so strikingly reveals that sense of guilt which pervades the long poem about his father included in this selection.

The function of poetry is therefore at once a liberation and a repression, and this is obvious from the first acknowledged poem Frénaud writes: *Epitaphe*. Like Yves Bonnefoy, he considers death as the starting point for existence, as the organic initiator for any renewal. Death, symbolically, becomes the lifegiver (as in Indian mythology). He has not stopped writing since that first epitaph. Was it the death of his father that was in question? Was it necessary to begin here before attempting any further acts that would illuminate his condition and make him aware of a truth that poetry succeeds in evoking? Decay and destruction are thus linked to mankind's condition, and it is through this transference, this objectification of his own most intimate emotions, expressed by means of universal images, that Frénaud manages to survive and to build a body of poetry that yet contains so many self-destructive elements. He began his ascension from that first poem out of the dark corridors of a past which he refused to specify. In breaking through to the verbal commitment, he found in poetry the tenuous security of liberation from obsessive guilt and sexual desires. The theme of the voyage, so frequently used by Frénaud, becomes symbolic of his effort to disengage himself, to feel, to go beyond, to attach himself to themes that would parallel his own search. Poems such as the long *Les Rois mages* (1943) are objective representations of his insecurity and of his recognition that security cannot be attained. (*Il n'y a pas de paradis*, as Frénaud has called one of his volumes.) The punishment is contained in this impossible ideal. Poetry becomes, in Michaux's terms, an exorcism, a safety factor. The poems reveal a pattern of trial and failure, endlessly repeated; an effort to reach a climax that never occurs. The voyage is a masochistic one, a trip of self-destruction as well as of cognition, discovering more and more about the complexity of attainment, about the equalization that slowly occurs between his own personal dilemma and its transmutation into a tragic theme pertaining to mankind proper. Out of this dejection he is able to construct a viable element—first of all, the poem itself, and then, the collection of poems that like a pilgrim's diary, describes his journey. Frénaud also recognizes that poetry is a shield from the ugliness within himself, and thus a deliverer (in his later poems he alludes more and more to a type of religious symbolism), although incapable of assuaging man's deepest anguish. This love-hate of poetry itself is the subject of one of the poems in this selection. Imbued with a Pascalian sense of man's fate, Frénaud proposes an Existential solution (he has been called a philosophic poet). Pitting Man against his Being allows the individual to arrive at a synthesis of his contradictions.

This double concern for mankind and for himself has given

Frénaud great liberty in the choice of his subjects; he has not only written about civic matters, but about mystical and erotic ones. Women, in fact, present a very complex concern in his poetry since they incarnate the ambiguous elements in life. They are both destruction and construction, Mother, Child and Wife simultaneously; they attract and they repel; they are physical: and how often has Frénaud been seduced by their presence? And they are spiritual, and here again Frénaud has felt their extreme significance.

There are fewer nuances when Frénaud deals specifically with men. Part Baudelaire-Rimbaud and part Marx (a frequent combination among French poets), Frénaud has elevated the proletariat to a symbol of man's dissatisfaction with the world. But the worker, like the poet, cannot free himself. There is a complicity between the poet and humanity, as there is also a skepticism about humanity's ultimate chances of success. This is evident in *L'Hôtel à plein sang*, and the refrain in *Les Rois mages*, where it is often Frénaud who speaks through the mask of his biblical characters that embody all of humanity's search. Yet the poem is no longer visibly determined by the poet himself; in the case of the longer poems, especially, it is clear that his personal condition has been metamorphosed.

Love, in this conception of mankind, becomes of ultimate consequence: it is the glimmer of hope, a possible resolution of man's tragic estate. It is Frénaud's own search, his own reaching, his own feeling of insecurity, his desire for brotherhood and sexual satisfaction; it is the recognition of a precarious unity in a situation that has always entailed solitude. But there are no absolute certainties, pleasure is never complete through the act of writing a poem, nor love ever taken to be a condition of beatitude. Man's failure prods him toward the female figure, enormous, with her breasts the objects of desire and also of hatred. *Aurore où toi et moi serons à jamais confondus* (Dawn where you and I will be eternally joined). The dialectic is once again set in motion as the poet rebels from this very statement, and like Orpheus, flees from his shadowy mother, symbolized by the Night, the Sea, the Earth, Being and Nothingness which attracts, embraces, dissolves, provides the warmth and the darkness for birth and for death. As Gide's Perseus might have said, after his father's death, Frénaud writes movingly:

Mon père depuis que tu es mort
c'est toi qui es devenu mon petit enfant.

Father since your death
you have become my little child.

The hated father becomes the child to be consoled. The father is the creator. With this formal substitution for God, Frénaud moves into a religious mysticism, reaching beyond the content of his emotions, and his relations with his mother and father, to attain another dimension.

The poet focuses on primary considerations: his relations to his parents, and his transformation of that basic theme into a richly woven tapestry that contains all the threads needed for a description of man himself. The father he destroyed and the father he is searching for become a fountain of inspiration, or, as the title of one of his poems indicates, an "irruption of words." Frénaud is not afraid to confront his demons nor to hope for peace. This "irruption of words," this feast to which he invites his reader, is the result of his Burgundian musicality, and his adroit mixture of the most prosaic language with the most colorful, the most precise and the most suggestive. With a variety of rhetorical devices, and a richness of tone and procedure, he strikes effectively on the responsive chords in man's constitution. Challenged by the world as it exists as much as by his own concerns, André Frénaud remains the true romantic, a poet who, conscious of religious, philosophic, social and political themes, succeeds in amalgamating them to his own personal visions.

Bonnefoy is a poet who has remarkably transcribed the tones of anguish and joy in terms that have frequently been regarded as falling into the domain of mysticism or metaphysics. He achieves this through a highly selective vocabulary composed of symbolic words —essential words—and a starkness like that of a well-cut stone that emits a light unerringly maintained in every poem. This incorruptible unity of style and thought excited the critics, who praised his work for its originality and the impression it made of having created a self-defined universe, different from other recent French poetry. The novelty was in part due to the almost immaterial imagery that etched out the discernible presence of Douve, the eponymous figure or image of his most famous book, and in part to the qualities ascribed to Douve that were so numerous and complex as to make the reader primarily aware of the illusiveness of her being. She is simultaneously a woman, thought, and nature.

Understandably, this projection of an inner experience, and the language in which it was couched, led to the accusation of over-intellectualization, a charge that might be leveled at all French poetry since Baudelaire. Bonnefoy is acutely sensitive to such a danger and he has categorically denied the possible refuge of a poem in pure form, as had both Valéry and Claudel.

Yet in the denial there is an admission, or at least a deep concern with a dilemma that is difficult to resolve: for Bonnefoy situates his reality in a context that refuses to accept pedestrian definitions of a highly personal vision. Thus, seeking to avoid abstract concepts and ideas, Bonnefoy calls upon the salamander as one of his examples of reality. And yet what could be further removed from what we consider reality than this alchemical figure, at once an allusion in the poetry of Scève (a sixteenth-century French poet), and an archetypal element in Bonnefoy's own poetics? The image-laden poems and the very words that he uses are thus as demanding in their relationship to reality as Douve herself.

This tension between levels of reality and our own apprehension of these levels contributes to an appreciation of one of the central problems that Bonnefoy investigates: the mediatory role as well as the limits of language as a means of describing essences, ultimate realities. His is truly a sort of metapoetics. This is clarified in one of his own critical essays "La poésie française et le principe d'identité" (*Un rêve fait à Mantoue*, Paris, Mercure de France, 1967), where he asserts that the poetic sense of a word, its connotative significance, is dissimilar to the linguistic treatment that examines non-poetic language, denotative language. For Bonnefoy, the word "fire" is not, as Saussure and his followers would have it, a semiological indication, but the totality of fire in the poet's own life. It is a thing that cannot be analyzed or utilized, that is therefore not of a finite and replaceable nature. The experience of fire should be similar to the experience one has when staring hard at an object: that object becomes diffused and then reforms to take on another aspect, interiorized and more essential than in its previous state. Fire thus suggests other things, linking, in the case of the poet, life and death, time and the viewer. It becomes the initiator of the experience rather than the object of the viewer's attention. Fire is equated to the idea of presence; it becomes, for an instant, indivisible from it.

Through this enrichment of meaning, the poem attains an inward reality; it becomes the discovery that binds the real world to the one the poet is describing. By choice, the poet substitutes essential words for superficial ones. The word "brick," for instance, has a number of conventional associations that are automatically evoked: it has a qualified image that has to be discarded in favor of, let us suppose, the word "stone" which is fundamental, which implies elementary being. It is this sort of selection that puts at the disposal of the poet a vocabulary specifically designed to serve his purpose. Out of words poetry will emerge. Mallarmé's injunction to his friend Degas becomes the base upon which Bonnefoy chooses to place his rival forces incarnated in vowels, consonants and the suggestive sense of the images themselves. The search is for a language capable of expressing the absolute; it is a way of breaking fixed meanings and thereby passing to a true experience of reality, as Rimbaud has done in his *Alchimie du Verbe*.

Bonnefoy's poetry is an eloquent testimony to the fact that this reality is not easily accessible. Though he wants to free himself from the dangers of abstraction, the haunting presence of concept hovers above the word like the spectre of the Platonic ideal, giving his poems a surrealist aura.

Death is at the junction between ideal and reality, between immobility and motion. In order not to be destroyed by his obsession with death, Bonnefoy conceives it as a productive force, a life-giving force, that allows him to live and to participate in the act of creation. Eliminating the fear of death, classifying it, naming it, the passage of life becomes assured, the abyss bridged, the present realized, as the poet, in a Thomistic act, enters the unnamable world where rationality is no longer the crutch on which poetic cognition rests.

The influence of Baudelaire is evident in this attitude toward death. Bonnefoy has written that Baudelaire invented death, and that he was also the poet who most clearly realized the enduring quality of the thing-in-itself, giving life to the moment and not to the idea or to the concept.

The resemblances between Bonnefoy and Baudelaire are striking, as are the differences in their treatment of their concerns. And yet, both poets share a common desire: to go beyond the façade of reality, to discover through words the world, where death is central not as the necessary finite expression but as the essential approach to the flux of life.

There are a number of indications of this in Bonnefoy's poetry. The wind is referred to as a messenger without a message, the annunciator of death, the forerunner, the initiator. Blood becomes the equivalent of life, the presence of immediate death, as the passage, the pulsation of the real. Much as the wind and blood carry the meaning of the ambiguous link between life and death, so do the myriad examples taken from the physical world and the vegetable kingdom.

Thus there are breaks in the ground, fissures in the architecture of the world, prescience of death—the fundamental axis upon which poetic movement is postulated. These indications occur at specific moments, on *le vrai lieu* (the true site), as he entitled one of the sections of *Douve*. It is at such moments that the sun strikes a window, and the poem, Janus-like, reveals its double identity for an instant, its past and its present, its silence and its fugacity. These are, furthermore, the moments when unnamed Voices take their place in the book. These otherwise untitled poems, firm as rocks, delineate the contours of their own presence and then merge in the neighboring landscape of other texts. This disappearance is the only means of transcending the here and the immediate. The Voice on the page makes a statement, and unravels a measure of the sense that has been evolving in poem after poem. In his quest for a *réalisme profond* to which poetry always reverts, the poet, guided by the evanescent stability of a Divine order, seeks in the *cœur sacré de l'instant* (the sacred heart of the instant) the certainty of the sudden act, the moral imperative worded in the language at his disposal. *Je voudrais que la poésie soit d'abord une incessante bataille, un théâtre où l'être et l'essence, la forme et le non-formel se combattront durement.** (I would want poetry to be first of all an inces-

* ("L'act et le lieu" in *L'Improbable*, Paris, Mercure de France, 1959, p. 176.)

sant battle, a theater where being and essence, form and the non-formal would struggle hard against each other.) Words become acts, leading to myths about what exists—leading, as Bonnefoy explains, to a negative theology. This pursuit is plotted out by the placement of objects that are at once specific and universal: wind, fire, earth, water—Tellurian spokesmen of another site, a God we do not know. Words are the very substance of that other and tenuous existence. In this, as in all poetic visions, language becomes our sole access to the profound meanings that recapture the "true site."

If Bonnefoy's *Douve* appears enigmatic, if these voices are representations of another and so often distant place, salvaged for a moment, and yet never wholly saved, André du Bouchet's work, equally slight in volume, reveals a number of evident resemblances despite notable differences in philosophic interests and idiographic usage. There is first du Bouchet's vocabulary which, according to Maurice Blanchot's definition, tends toward abstraction: night, death, earth, being. His is not a proliferating vocabulary expanding to meet the needs of his invention; rather, with monastic severity, he has divested himself of all the words that would make harder an already difficult task. The language at his disposal is not the high language of classic poetry, but the inferences this language allows him are not irrelevant to Bonnefoy's own pursuits.

Bonnefoy, by comparison, appears more feminine—as *Douve* is feminine—but du Bouchet is also, from another, more earthly direction, equally ready to grant a degree of independence to the obverse of reality, to that other side which is infrequently captured by Bonnefoy, though it is his main objective. This obverse of reality also eludes du Bouchet, who also travels a road (a frequent image) toward an undefined source, thereby creating the forceful paradox of a presence in its absence.

This pursuit of an absence reminds us of Mallarmé's anguish over the white page, and Mallarmé's *Un coup de dés n'abolira jamais le hasard* has exerted a powerful influence on both Bonnefoy and du Bouchet.

Indicative of this Mallarméan influence is du Bouchet's penchant for the visual presentation of his metaphysical concerns: the page is all-menacing, and on it, the few scattered words, like stones or seeds, interrupt the overpowering negation of the absolute whiteness. Each line, continuous or broken, appears as an affirmation, a precious statement, compiling the very mountain that is the subject of the poem—"climbing to the unknown," as Jean-Pierre Richard has observed.

With these few glyphs of the poet's meaning cautiously placed on the page, the traction of the poem proceeds, defining the quest for light and meaning through the elaboration of itself. This is also germane to Mallarmé's concepts and much in favor among the younger poets who consider that the poem itself offers the best mechanism toward elaboration of a manifest structure, regardless of its sense in the traditional manner. The text that is spread out between the two polarities of beginning and end, whether accessible or hermetic, represents a concerted effort to plot out with language itself the structures of our thoughts, the undefined presences that we seek to uncover and clarify.

Thus the light comes not only from the word itself, but also from the brilliance of the pages swallowing the text as it begins to assume a shape, as it forcefully advances. As the desert consumes all that is liquid, so the light consumes all matter, leaving only the mysterious wind, transcendental, arising out of the object, and achieving a sort of universal reality no longer immediately representational.

The title of one of du Bouchet's long poems is *Le Moteur blanc*, signifying this propulsion, this whiteness generated by extreme heat, invisible as the *Chaleur vacante*, the title of another collection of poems. In actuality, what crosses the day is the day itself, in its diurnal passage. It does not see itself—it is in motion. In this substance-less landscape, lunar, transparent, single objects—trees, fields, individuals, walls—proceed as if they were in a Chirico world, fragile, timeless, yet filled with the impossibility that we see in the broken lines of the poems. This is a carefully unsettling world, stripped, with distant fires, and many roads that cut the poem, like the very lines into which the poem is divided. On this stage there is a solitary man who walks with difficulty, passes through, as a visitor—and we accompany him. There are no needless harmonies encountered, there are only gestures, a look, a few inscriptions on the page that testify to the tensions, to the revelatory process out of which images like messages are emitted.

These semiological presences reveal a sequential aspiration that is both determined by the left-right reading pattern and by the syntactical play which provokes the reader into accepting du Bouchet's wanderings in this Waste Land. Yet the desert does have an exit: what seems to be impassable, like so many of du Bouchet's obstacles, disappears as it is confronted. There are countless passages through his poetry, some made of space, others made of air underlying the attraction-repulsion principle that generates the movement of the poem and the direction of the poet himself.

Writing becomes an act of provocation, like breathing in the air, which for du Bouchet entails putting into motion a countervailing force. More fundamentally, the poem becomes a surgical statement revealing its wounds and the art of writing, both facets of existence. And it is in this manner that his poetry, far from appearing as an act of desperation, as a negation, avows its success in the composition, in the transcendence of the matter of the poem. Within the poem, eliminating the contradiction between the place of departure and the anticipated goal, the poet admits the similarity of place between where he stands and where he seeks to go. The road is both obstacle and continuity, the here-and-now as well as the distance itself.

This conclusion absolves the poet from temporality; it assures him of the eternal presence within himself, beginning and ending at its starting point, but also denying the efficacy of the constant autodestruction, since the poem itself moves forward imperturbably, impeded but never permanently blocked by the white abysses that the phrases must bridge. Typography and topography. The syntax contributes to this effort, adding impossible simultaneities that provoke a sort of dizziness in the viewer who then can "see" the logic of the poem, a poem which has determined the ground upon which it must be read and understood. The poem is consequently both an escape from being and a constant interpretation by the realities noted: day, fire, walls, room, bed, hand. It is a desperate act of reacting, fulfilled in the writing, and once ended, unsatisfactory, except as another demonstration of the presence of the poet.

The poem as confrontation between poet and text is nowhere as evident as in the case of the two youngest contributors to this selection: Marcelin Pleynet and Denis Roche. Whereas Bonnefoy and du Bouchet, Frénaud, Guillevic and Follain represent distinct, even though not always dissimilar, interpretations of the meaning and direction of poetry, the texts composed by Denis Roche and Marcelin Pleynet, in the vanguard of today's poetry, provide a definite indication of the joining of Surrealism with Pongian esthetics.

Both these influences, as well as a number of subsidiary ones taken from contemporary writers frequently outside the realm of literature, have contributed to the formulation of a poetic statement that emphasizes, sometimes brutally, an intellectual effort that denies the usual transcription.

This paradox, which works so well in the finely wrought poems in *Douve*, appears in the works of Pleynet and Roche to take on a rather cold-blooded aspect, closer to the post-mortem operations of some of the structuralist analyses of literary texts than to the materialization of a human substance that is found in the work of a Frénaud, for instance.

There are at least two basic tenets that are shared by Pleynet and Roche and that explain in part the character of their poetry, otherwise not alike either in choice of language, syntax or visual disposition. The first is a recognition of the significance of the structures that underlie the act of writing. This implies a conscious participation on the part of the poet in the unconscious deliberations that amount to the poem as it is being composed. Nothing exists but in its verbal sense: and thus the poem mentioning a tree does not allude to any other reality but to the tree that is evoked by the word. It is not a careless or innocent effort to duplicate the natural object by naming it, as the Romantics had practiced; neither is it a lyrical use of the image that would provoke in the reader some suggestion of a world outside of the poem that exists essentially by itself.

The second tenet, allied to the first, is the recognition that if the unconscious operates with such effectiveness and such importance, as the Surrealists had noted, and if the function of the analogy is to provide a fortuitous combination that would exalt linguistic expressions, then it is up to the poet to capitalize on this interior ferment, and compose in such a manner as to grant independence to language as it emerges.

Denis Roche, far less committed, then, to the idealization of thought, far less intrigued by the solution of "philosophic" problems, apparently unconcerned with the exploitation of traditional Baudelairian thematics, or even Rimbaldian ones, has tried to reconstruct the very pattern of the reading-writing symbiosis, especially in his *Les idées centésimales de Miss Elanize.* Here the poet forces the reader to undergo an experience that is irritating and meaningless according to previous standards of critical judgements—judgements rendered according to an unquestioned faith in the logical progression of ideas that encourage the reader, in spite of the genre, to piece together the "story" of the poem. In Roche's own formula, there is a constantly interrupted play of fantastic meanings that appear like recognizable prose but which, in reality, as Robbe-Grillet points out in *Les Gommes*, must be understood as a series of hieroglyphic annotations, the secret of which is withheld from those who are not initiated into the new style of reading, into the new understanding of the significance of the act of writing taken as a self-evidence, with no allusions, with no predetermined concept at its root that must be demonstrated and rationally explained. As Robbe-Grillet strips the novel of its distinguishing features, using a murder mystery to present his views on both his art and the physical construction of the novel itself—so Denis Roche, in his apparently compact poems which he would prefer to call texts (as would most of the structuralist-oriented poets) insists on a conventional visual presentation that will play off the Breton-like appearance of freely associated ideas. These provide the syntactical clues to the solution of a thought, and is no more or less than the line itself, self-contained, without any deliberate desire on the poet's part to extend the meaning beyond the language it has established so rigorously on each page. These rich, unpremeditated, ironic, vibrant lines become the "centesimal ideas of Miss Elanize." We are increasingly made aware that what counts is the recognition of the particular qualities of thinking and writing, as a model or a form, and that it is only after the reader has acknowledged this factor that he can begin to piece the lines together, to forge interlocking movements familiar to the linguist.

At no time, then, have young writers been as heedful of the constitutive parts of their craft: the word and by extension the largest unit possible, the phrase itself. This conviction in formal terms has resulted in an axial change in the artists' perspective, leading them, as has traditionally been the case in France, to discover an historical justification by reinterpreting writers of the past, or living ones in a different manner, who could be shown to have concerns similar to their own.

Thus, Lautréamont, Sade, Raymond Roussel, André Breton, Mallarmé and Flaubert have been carefully reconsidered, and found to share, first, a radicalization of an anti-bourgeois stance (political, sexual, linguistic), and secondly, a highly evolved sense of the autonomy of language. Or, as Flaubert would have it, of the phrase, which (apart from its content here envisaged as a pure fabrication serving to invest the text with beauty) poses problems singularly pertinent to words themselves. Roland Barthes has said that, in those concerns so forthrightly communicated in his correspondence, Flaubert had gone beyond the nineteenth century's concern for style, and had become the first to consider, in utmost lucidity, the next level, the positivist level as Comte would say, where language itself and its grammatical and tonal definitions become of primary interest.

Marcelin Pleynet has characterized the essence of his confrontation with language in the following pseudo-formal declaration:

I. ON NE PEUT PAS SAVOIR ÉCRIRE SANS SAVOIR POURQUOI.
(One cannot know how to write without knowing why.)

II. L'AUTEUR DE CET ART POÉTIQUE NE SAIT COMMENT ÉCRIRE MAIS IL ÉCRIT.
(The author of this ars poetica does not know how to write but he writes.)

III. LA QUESTION "COMMENT ÉCRIRE" RÉPOND À LA QUESTION "POURQUOI ÉCRIRE" ET À LA QUESTION "QU'EST-CE QUE L'ÉCRITURE".
(The question "how to write" answers the question "why write" and the question "what is writing.")

IV. UNE QUESTION EST UNE RÉPONSE.
(A question is an answer.)*

This elaboration provides the key to Pleynet's *Provisoires amants des nègres* (Ed. du Seuil, 1962), where, in an effort similar to Roche's, Pleynet assumes that the poem exists and then disappears as one turns every page. There is also, in his paraphrasing of Rimbaud's *Je est un nègre*, the Surrealist play, the humor and the construction that allows

---

* *Tel quel*, hiver, 1964, Number 16, p. 3.

the reader, once he has gone through and along the skeletal frame of language, to assume, as does Pleynet, the existence, somewhere imbedded in the poem, of a drama, of a ritual, which is part verbal, part landscape. This concern is taken a step further in *Paysages en deux* and *Les Lignes de la prose* jointly published in 1963, where the intentional landscape becomes language conscious of itself, as well as conscious of its possible acts of rapprochement with reality, an effort that leads Pleynet to criticize subjective language in order to restore language to its proper function: that of communication and truth which it would lose were it not for the restructuring of its elements by the poet within the confines of a poetic space.

One of the problems, then, that confronts a number of the younger poets and critics is a matter of definition and re-orientation. They must challenge the classifications that have afflicted literature and led the untutored reader into believing that there was such a thing as Poetry with a capital P—poetry as an ideal, lofty in its aspirations toward a world that had Truth stamped on it, and honor on its banner, a poetry sheltered from the rest of linguistic experience shared by other non-literary disciplines.

In order to deny the validity of blindly accepted cultural norms or clichés that have imposed a double standard when dealing with reality—one having to do with "nature" and the other one with "writing"—poets today have forced the issue on the formalist plane in order to uncover and evaluate the actual mechanism that constitutes the writing experience. In effect, they have denied the separateness of poetry from the other genres, and have sought to provide a system of evaluation that would be applicable to all forms of written communication, whether in the arts, the social sciences, or presumably even in the pure sciences.

The result is an arduous combat within contemporary French culture. André Breton once declared that to the Surrealist there was no difference between Marx's injunction to transform the world and Rimbaud's declaration that it was equally necessary to change life itself. Basing themselves on Breton's declaration, such as the importance of Freud (*Genèse et perspective artistique du surréalisme*), or that it is necessary to begin anew from the word itself (*Les mots sans rides*) and, more eloquently stated in his second Surrealist manifesto, that it is imperative to provoke a *crise de conscience* that would affect both the moral, the intellectual and the esthetic norms, these young writers have found in the Structuralist methodology a means of achieving their independence from the accumulated burdens of French culture.

Having found this method and taking their cue from the triple inspiration of Marx, Freud and Lévi-Strauss they have discovered a precursor in Lautréamont, a vital magazine in *Tel quel*, and a living elder statesman in Francis Ponge. With this intellectual equipment, and an almost religious conviction in the rightness of their beliefs, they have begun a salutory revision of the interpretation of the dominant themes of Western civilization.

SERGE GAVRONSKY

Francis Ponge

Born 1899 in Montpellier

In the month of July, at eleven o'clock, drinking scotch in Provence, in a garden overlooking two hundred olive trees that belong to Francis Ponge. The poet is at home in his renovated farmer's house, newly painted, and situated on the side of a hill that dominates the horizon. His grandchildren yell on the swings: his wife and daughter watch over them. He sits near a singular palm tree, identifying the plants and flowers of the region. As he speaks (and he had spoken similarly the night before when we drove to Antibes in the dark), every word seems to fit the qualities of the thing described. Without any apparent effort, Francis Ponge evokes his surroundings with the precision of a writer who is supremely aware of the need for accuracy. This is done with the same admiration for details that is generally accorded to Fabre or Buffon, and in a style as perfectly suitable. But the precision is not limited to natural objects. As we walk through the Picasso Museum and later the Maeght Foundation, commenting on the Chagalls and the Giacomettis, Ponge qualifies with the same acuity. Such is the conviction with which he speaks that even a banal observation has a particular resonance to it: he is conscious of his words, as he is of his past and of his presence.

Francis Ponge is a small, stocky and well-built man, bald as a Roman bust, enjoying the accolades that have recently been bestowed on him. His pride is exemplary, in the manner of a seventeenth-century Frondeur. One knows that he considers his works as already beyond question, assimilated to the body of French literature. But he has also lived too long in obscurity not to find this belated recognition somewhat inconsequential. His poems and texts had gained the admiration of Valéry, and after the war, Sartre and Camus both praised them. To the "happy few," then, Ponge never needed introduction, though financially, as a teacher at the Alliance française, it could not have been an easy life. But parallel to this existence, he fashioned his poetic objects pitching his voice to their keys. Such were the arduous tasks the writer had set before himself. The war did not outwardly affect his work. Patriot and nationalist, Ponge wrote poems that could not specifically be ascribed to the moment: everything that he had believed in excluded the historical moment, the condescension to a particular time. In the sixties, when he was discovered by a new generation, his esthetic principles had not changed.

Ponge stands on flat pebbled ground giving me directions on how to best manoeuver up the slight and irregular path that goes from his house to the paved road up ahead. Language could not be more handsomely illustrated nor could any poet be found who might better be entrusted with its defense.

Would you place yourself in the current of French poetry since 1945?

I am obviously much older than that, since I began publishing in the '20's, and even during the first years of the '20's. I wrote *Parti pris des choses* between 1926 and 1935, though it was not published until 1942, and then it was only slightly known through articles and Sartre's essay, which dates from 1944–45. Consequently, we begin more or less at the time I had gained a measure of notoriety. I was only then known by the Happy Few.

My position in French literary history does not begin in 1945—that is well known. My reaction against poetry the way I found it when I appeared on the scene, when I began writing, was an anti-lyrical reaction. It so happens that this fact only began to be understood rather late. This is in part due to Surrealism which is essentially lyrical and which was still very important, and equally, in 1945, to patriotic poetry, which was also strongly lyrical at that time. It was only due to the emergence of things like the philosophy of phenomenology that my poetry was recognized. In fact, I have never wanted to, strictly speaking, and this I repeat at every occasion, I have never wanted to "write poetry," to constitute poetic objects, if you want, in the habitual sense of the word. I write as I write, and I do not want it to be poetry. I do not intend to write poems. I express my feelings about things that move me, or that seem to me to be important to state. I have protested at length against my classification among poets, because lyricism in general disturbs me. That is, it seems to me there is something too subjective, a display of subjectivity which appears to me to be unpleasant, slightly immodest. I believe that things—how can I say it—that emanate from your own subjectivity, should not be displayed. Naturally, one never does anything but that. My own resolution was rather to reverse the situation and to try to say things that were generally valuable and pertinent. That is the reason why I have chosen things, objects, so that I would always have a brake on my subjectivity, calling back the object as it exists when I write about it. So that I would not write: "I love apples" but I would try to describe the apple—that's it. And if I allow myself to say that the apple is savory, well, I would bring into play other qualities of the apple to substantiate the apple to the detriment of my simple taste or love of the object. That is to say, objects represent a way of freeing myself from my subjectivity. At least I try, I know that it is not entirely feasible. I am not mad enough to believe that the apple expresses itself when I speak. Nevertheless, I force myself to add to the qualities of the apple certain qualities that come from it and not from me. I think that at the same time I change my own subjectivity. That is, I believe that when one loves someone, or something, one must love it for what it is, and not for what it appears to be to you. First of all, it is necessary to let it live. I try to allow the object to live rather than simply stating my own sentiments about it.

But I have moved away from your question which was my position in poetry since 1945. It is a position, which was first, as I have told you, in contradiction to the poetic mainstream of the times, and which, little by little, nevertheless, made its way, and for example, I have never written poems that were patriotic declarations or that were invectives against the enemy of the period: the Nazis. It so happens that a few of my poems, such as the *Lessiveuse* were considered as patriotic poems. Why? I was probably imbued with patriotism, and it appeared without my wanting it in the texts that I was writing. So that I participated in the publications of patriotic poetry but my poetry was absolutely—my texts, if you want—were entirely different from those that appeared in those editions. That is, their subject matter did not pertain to patriotism. And then, in 1945, in France, first of all there was this continuation of the influence of the great Surrealist poets who had taken an active part in the Resistance, and who had become patriotic poets, like Eluard and Aragon. They continued to have disciples. And afterwards, the rise of Char, who had equally been active in the Resistance and who had also been a Surrealist, as you know, but whose poetry was completely different. It is not my intention to analyze Char's poetry, or that of the others—only to point out that the ones who were emerging were Char, Artaud through another way, and Prévert through a completely different way, and that my own poetry was considered anti-poetic, which pleased me perfectly, since I was absolutely in agreement with that judgment, given the fact that at that time there was either song or more frequently, eloquence. As a consequence, and to a degree, I remained "hidden" from view. Though I was certainly being read, I was not being published in the fashionable magazines of the day.

It is only later, in the '60's, slightly earlier, when a new school, the one associated with *Tel quel* leaned a little on me, that I found these very young men (they were all between 20 and 30 years old), interested in what I was doing in the same way that they considered writers who were not, strictly speaking, poets, like Georges Bataille or precisely Artaud and whose interest led them to the Surrealism of Breton rather than the one that had been expressed by Eluard or Aragon. As far as history is concerned, I think that is about all that I have to say: I was first taken up by the Classicists, men of the *Nouvelle Revue Française* who published me when I was young in 1925, and then by Sartre and the Existentialists and by Camus because of my "phenomenological" side. And finally, by this young school for reasons which seem to be more profoundly valuable since it was not attracted by traditional aspects of poetry but exactly by my anti-lyricism, my taste for a poetry or texts closer to science, and pertaining to the linguistic aspects of poetry.

Would you care to discuss the ways in which you select words?

Yes. Words come, if you will, in a host, as soon as one touches what I call the sensitive chord of each thing. Let us take an example, a metaphor. It seems to me that the breath of speaking, the animus, can be compared in part to natural breath, let us say, the wind, and the wind makes things vibrate, trees as well as chimneys. But the problem is to make our breath vibrate each thing according to its own particular timbre. I don't know if this is a game played in the United States, but young boys in France like to blow into a bottle until they find its particular key. Each thing, each being, each landscape, each esthetic composition has a moment when it rings accurately. That pitch has got to be found. When it is found, and that is what I attempt to do, words are selected according to their adequacy to this chord. Naturally, the phonetic quality, the phoneme, what I call the concert of syllables, is more often chosen on the basis of this, according to the sensitive chord, which is the difference itself, than to its significance properly speaking. This explains at once both the difficulty and the fascinating interest of the word taken as a means of expression: instead of its being color as in the case of painters, or articulated sounds as in the case of music. So that it is truly a question of arriving at an equality between significance and the phonetic value. Inescapably, one must consider the sense—it would be impossible not to do otherwise. Words already have a definition, which must be taken into account. I play simultaneously on the sense and on the musical quality of the syllabic word, the syllabic concert. Here is the area of difficulty. Consequently, those words that are excluded are those whose sense does not—no, let us say rather whose syllabic value, whose musical value—does not approximate the sense. For example, I would chose words that would be perhaps less significant as far as the dictionary definition is concerned, but which would be closer to the general tonality that I have sought out in my text, because they seem to me to correspond (this is a subjective thing) to my impression of the thing in itself. When I say that *cruche* is deeper than the word *creux*, it is because the *u* forces the mouth to open, and therefore makes a sound deeper than *creux*. The shape or form must also be taken into account, because the visual image of the word also counts for a lot. And not only do we speak, but we write, and writing is a thing that falls in the domain of vision, and since printing, poets have been sensitive—the artists of the word have been as sensitive—to the scriptural value, to the shape of the word, its form, the word and the written letter, as they have been to its phonetic value. As you can see, there is the sense of the word, there is its visual value and there is its audible value. All that is very difficult to combine. After all, it is only a word. I reject what does not function and I accept only those words that work in these three dimensions.

What part does Latin etymology play in this selection?

Latin allows me to play specifically on the definitions, the dictionary meanings, that are older, more elementary. I wish my texts to be respectful of the etymological origins of words. And Latin is clearly the basis of much of the etymology of French words. My choice also represents a wariness in the reading as you can see: I don't hold much faith in a reading of my texts according to contemporary definitions of words. The text has got to be anchored to the thickest definition, the deepest one, consequently the original definition. The best would be to incorporate all the successive definitions of the word during its semantical history, and in the dictionary this is represented by the first, second and third meanings of each word, revealing how words have varied in their definitions. This often corresponds to a history, to their definition in history, because the same Latin roots have been given successive meanings, and derivations of these words are different, for example, in Italian, Spanish, Rumanian, French or Provençal. Thus, history, as it operates through time, is something that one must heed. As for their definitions, the ultimate would be in finding the propriety of the term, as it used to be said in the seventeenth century, and as it is still being said, finding in each sentence, in each paragraph, in the whole text, all the semantic levels, all the successive definitions, beginning with its roots, simultaneously respected. Naturally, that is an impossible expectation, but to consider it does allow one to arrive at a certain thickness, at a degree of certitude of the propriety of the terms involved. One has to ask the most in order to obtain the least. It is an impossible absolute that all words, that the texts, be written in such a way as to allow the words their complete semantical thickness. This is impossible. But if one has that sensitivity to the thickness of words, to the fact that they do have a history, that they have provoked associations of different ideas in each language and in each of the periods of the evolution of language, then this provides a much thicker material, graver, much graver in the sense of weight, a material that is not superficial, which is a thing that one can mold precisely because it has the quality, the thickness, of potter's clay. It is a physical object with many dimensions.

PRINCIPAL WORKS: *Le Parti pris des choses*, Gallimard, 1942
Dix-courts sur la Méthode, Seghers, 1946
Proèmes, Gallimard, 1948
Le Peintre à l'étude, Gallimard, 1948
La Seine, Clairfontaine, 1950
Le Grand Recueil (3 vols.), Gallimard, 1961
Pour un Malherbe, Gallimard, 1965
Nouveau Recueil, Gallimard, 1967
Le Savon, Gallimard, 1967

Le Soleil lu à la radio

I

Puisque tel est le pouvoir du langage,
Battrons-nous donc soleil comme princes monnaie,
Pour en timbrer le haut de cette page?
L'y ferons-nous monter comme il monte au zénith?

OUI

Pour qu'ainsi réponde, au milieu de la page,
L'acclamation du monde à son exclamation!

2

«Brillant soleil adoré du Sauvage...»
Ainsi débute un chœur de l'illustre Rameau.
Ainsi, battons soleil comme l'on bat tambour!
Battons soleil aux champs! Battons la générale!

OUI

Battons d'un seul cœur pavillon du soleil!

3

Pourtant, tel est le pouvoir du langage,
Que l'Ombre aussi est en notre pouvoir.
Déjà, prenons-y garde,
Le soleil la comporte et ce *oui* la contient:
OUI, je viens dans son temple adorer l'Éternel.
OUI, c'est Agamemnon, c'est ton roi qui t'éveille!
Par la même exclamation monosyllabique
Débute la Tragédie.
OUI, l'Ombre ici déjà est en pouvoir.

Reading the Sun on Radio

1

Since such is the power of language,
Shall we then mint the sun as princes do money,
To stamp the top of this page?
Shall we make it climb as it climbs to the zenith?

YES

So that the answer may be in the middle of the page,
The acclamation of the world to its exclamation!

2

"Brilliant sun adored by the Savage . . ."
Thus begins a chorus by the illustrious Rameau.
Thus, let us beat the sun as we beat a drum!
Let us beat the praises of the sun! Beat the alarum!

YES

Let us beat with a common heart the colors of the sun!

3

But, such is the power of language,
That the Shadow is also in our power
Already, let us beware,
The sun allows it and this *yes* contains it:
YES, I enter his temple to adore the Eternal.
YES, it is Agamemnon, it is your king who awakens you!
With the same monosyllabic exclamation
The Tragedy begins.
YES, the Shadow here is already in power.

4

Nous ne continuerons donc pas sur ce ton.

La révolte, comme l'acclamation, est facile.

Mais voici peut-être le point.

Qu'est-ce que le soleil comme objet?—C'est le plus brillant des objets du monde.

OUI, brillant à tel point! Nous venons de le voir.

Il y faut tout l'orchestre: les tambours, les clairons, les fifres, les tubas. Et les tambourins, et la batterie.

Tout cela pour dire quoi?—Un seul monosyllabe. Une seule onomatopée monosyllabique.

Le soleil ne peut être remplacé par aucune formule logique, CAR le soleil n'est pas un objet.

LE PLUS BRILLANT des objets du monde n'est—de ce fait—NON—*n'est pas* un objet; c'est un trou, c'est l'abîme métaphysique: la condition formelle et indispensable de tout au monde. La condition de tous les autres objets. La condition même du regard.

5

Et voici ce qui en lui est atroce. Vraiment, du dernier mauvais goût! Vraiment, qui nous laisse loin de compte, et nous empêche de l'adorer:

Cette condition *sine qua non* de tout ce qui est au monde s'y montre, s'y impose, y apparaît.

Elle a le front de s'y montrer!

Qui plus est, elle s'y montre de telle façon qu'elle interdit qu'on la regarde, qu'elle repousse le regard, vous le renfonce à l'intérieur du corps!

Vraiment, quel tyran!

Non seulement, il nous oblige *à être*, je vais dire dans quelles conditions—mais il nous force à le contempler—et cependant nous en empêche, nous interdit de le fixer.

OUI et NON!

C'est un tyran et un artiste, un artificier, un acteur! Néron! Ahenobarbus!

4

We shall not, therefore, carry on this way.

Revolt, like acclamation, is easy.

But perhaps that's the point.

What kind of object is the sun?—it is the brightest object in the world.

YES, brilliant to a degree! we have just seen its brilliance.

A whole orchestra is needed: drums, bugles, fifes, tubas. And the tambourines and the timpani.

Meaning what?—A single monosyllable. A single onomatopoetic monosyllable.

The sun cannot be replaced by any logical formula, FOR the sun is not an object.

THE BRIGHTEST of all objects in the world is—consequently —NOT—*is not* an object; it is a void, the metaphysical abyss: the formal and indispensable condition of everything in the world. The condition of all other objects. The condition of sight itself.

5

And this is what is atrocious about it. Really the last word in bad taste! What leaves us really unsatisfied, and stops us from adoring it:

This *sine qua non* condition of everything in the world is revealed in it, is imposed by it, appears in it.

It has the effrontery to show itself!

What's more, it reveals itself in such a way that it stops you from looking at it, that it repulses the look, pushing it back into the interior of the body!

A real tyrant!

Not only does it force us *to be*, I will say later under what conditions—but it forces us to contemplate it—and nevertheless stops us from doing so, stops us from staring at it.

YES and NO!

It's a tyrant and an artist, a conjurer, an actor! Nero! Ahenobarbus!

6

Voici en quelques mots ce qui s'est passé.

Le Soleil, qui n'est pas la Vie, qui est peut-être la Mort (comme Gœthe l'a décrite: «plus de lumière»), qui est sans doute en deçà de la Vie et de la Mort,—a expulsé de Lui certaines de ses parties, les a exilées, envoyées à une certaine distance pour s'en faire contempler.

Envoyées, dis-je, à une certaine distance. Distance fort bien calculée. Suffisante pour qu'elles refroidissent, suffisante pour que ces exilées aient assez de recul pour le contempler. Insuffisante pour qu'elles échappent à son attraction et ne doivent continuer autour de lui leur ronde, leur service de spectateurs.

Ainsi elles refroidissent, car il les a vouées à la mort, mais d'abord—et c'est bien pire—à cette maladie, à cette tiédeur que l'on nomme la vie. Et, par exemple, quant à l'homme, à ses trente-sept degrés centigrades. Ah ! Songez combien plus proche de la mort est la vie, cette tiédeur, que du soleil et de ses milliards de degrés centigrades !

J'en dirais autant des formes et des couleurs, qui expriment la damnation particulière de chaque être, de chaque spectateur exilé du soleil. Sa damnation, c'est-à-dire sa façon particulière d'adorer et de mourir.

7

Ainsi les corps et la vie même ne sont qu'une dégradation de l'énergie solaire, vouée à la contemplation et au regret de celle-ci, et—presque aussitôt—à la mort.

Ainsi le soleil est un fléau. Voyez : comme les fléaux, il fait éclater les épis, les cosses. Mais c'est un fléau sadique, un fléau médecin. Un fléau qui fait se reproduire et qui entretient ses victimes ; qui les *recrée* et s'en fait désirer.

Car—cet objet éblouissant—un nuage, un écran, le moindre volet, la moindre paupière qu'il forme suffit à le cacher, et donc à le faire désirer. Et il ne manque pas d'en former. Et ainsi la moitié de la vie se passe-t-elle dans l'ombre, à souhaiter la chaleur et la lumière, c'est-à-dire les travaux forcés dans la prison de l'azur.

6

Here in a few words is what happened.

The Sun, which is not Life, which is perhaps Death (as Goethe described it: "more light"), which is without a doubt beyond Life and Death,—expelled from Itself certain fragments, exiled them, sent them a certain distance in order to be contemplated by them.

Sent out, I say, a certain distance. A well-calculated distance. Sufficient that they grow cold, sufficient so that these exiles have enough perspective to contemplate it. Insufficient for them to escape its attraction, and to stop circling around it, as dutiful spectators.

Thus, they grow cold, for it has destined them to die, but first—which is much worse— to this sickness, to this tepidity called life. And, in the case of man, to these ninety-eight point six degrees. Ah! Think of how much closer to death is life, this tepidity, than it is to the sun and to its millions of degrees Fahrenheit!

I would say as much about the forms and colors that express the particular damnation of each being, of each spectator exiled from the sun. Each damnation, that is to say, each particular way of adoring and dying.

7

Thus bodies and life itself are but a degradation of solar energy, destined to contemplate it and to regret it, and—almost at once—to die.

Thus, the sun is a flail. Behold: Like flail, it breaks open the spears of grain, the husks. But it is a sadistic scourge, a remedial scourge. A scourge that encourages reproduction and watches over its victims; that *recreates* them and makes itself desired.

For—this blinding object—a cloud, a screen, the thinnest shade, the thinnest eyelid that it forms suffices to hide it and therefore to make it desirable. And it does not fail to form them. And thus half of life is spent in the shade, wishing for heat and light, that is to say forced labor in a prison of azure.

8

Pourtant, voici que cette fable comporte une moralité.

Car, plongés dans l'ombre et dans la nuit par les caprices du soleil et sa coquetterie sadique, les objets éloignés de lui au service de le contempler, tout à coup voient le ciel étoilé.

Il a dû les éloigner de lui pour qu'ils le contemplent (et se cacher à eux pour qu'ils le désirent), mais voici qu'ils aperçoivent alors ces myriades d'étoiles, les myriades d'*autres* soleils.

Et il n'a pas fallu longtemps pour qu'ils les comptent. Et ne comptent leur propre soleil *parmi* l'infinité des astres, non comme le plus important. Le plus proche et le plus tyrannique, certes.

Mais enfin, l'un seulement des soleils.

Et je ne dis pas qu'une telle considération les rassure, mais elle les venge...

9

Ainsi, plongé dans le désordre absurde et de mauvais goût du monde, dans le chaos inouï des nuits, l'homme du moins compte les soleils.

Mais enfin, son dédain s'affirme et il cesse même de les compter.

(*Écrit le XXII juin de ma cinquante et unième année: jour du solstice d'été.*)

10

... Cependant le soleil se fait longuement regretter; nuit et nuées; s'éloigne de la terre, conçue vers le solstice d'hiver.

Puis il remonte.

C'est alors qu'il faut continuer par l'expression de la remontée du soleil, malgré nous. Et, bien sûr, cela ne peut finir que par un nouveau désespoir, accru («Encore un jour qui luit!»).

Il ne reste donc qu'*une* solution.

Recommencer volontairement l'hymne. Prendre décidément le soleil en bonne part. C'est aussi là le pouvoir du langage. Nous en féliciter, réjouir. L'en féliciter. L'honorer, le chanter,

8

However, there is a moral to this story.

For, plunged in the shade and the night by the sun's caprice and its sadistic whims, objects placed at a certain distance in order to contemplate it, suddenly see the starry sky.

It had to place them at a distance in order to be contemplated by them (and to hide itself from them in order to be desired), but now they see these myriad stars, these myriad *other* suns.

And it did not take them long to count them. And to count their own sun *among* an infinity of stars, and not as the most important. Although the closest and the most tyrannical.

But finally, only one among the suns.

And I do not say that such a consideration reassures them, but it avenges them . . .

9

Thus plunged in the absurd disorder and bad taste of the world, in the incredible chaos of nights, man at least counts the suns.

But finally, his disdain affirms itself and he even stops counting them.

(*Written June XXII of my fifty-first year: the day of the summer solstice.*)

10

. . . However, the sun has itself regretted for a long time; night and clouds; moves away from the earth, conceived at the time of the winter solstice.

Then it rises again.

Then it is necessary to continue tracking the ascent of the sun, despite ourselves. And naturally, this can only end up in a new despair, sharpened ("Still another day that shines!")

There is, then, only *one* solution left.

Start the hymn voluntarily again. Take the sun in good faith. That is also in the power of language. Congratulate ourselves, rejoice

tâchant seulement de *renouveler* les thèmes (et variations) de ce los. Le nuancer, en plein ravissement.

Certes nous savons à quoi nous en tenir, mais *à tout prix* la santé, la réjouissance et la joie.

Il faut donce métalogiquement le «refaire», le posséder.

En plein ravissement.

«Remonte donc, puisque enfin tu remontes. Tu me recrées. Ah! j'ai médit de toi! Etc..., etc.»

Changer le mal en bien. Les travaux forcés en Paradis.

Puis finir dans l'ambiguïté hautement dédaigneuse, ironique et tonique à la fois; le fonctionnement verbal, sans aucun coefficient laudatif ni péjoratif: l'objeu.

Éclaircie en hiver

Le bleu renaît du gris, comme la pulpe éjectée d'un raisin noir.

Toute l'atmosphère est comme un œil trop humide, où raisons et envie de pleuvoir ont momentanément disparu.

Mais l'averse a laissé partout des souvenirs qui servent au beau temps de miroirs.

Il y a quelque chose d'attendrissant dans cette liaison entre deux états d'humeur différente. Quelque chose de désarmant dans cet épanchement terminé.

Chaque flaque est alors comme une aile de papillon placée sous vitre,

Mais il suffit d'une roue de passage pour en faire jaillir de la boue.

about it. Congratulate it. Honor it, sing to it, trying only to *renovate* the themes (and variations) of the gramercy. Be subtle, in the midst of this rapture.

Obviously we know what to expect, but *at all cost* health, pleasure and joy.

Therefore, it is necessary "to do it over," metalogically to possess it.

In the midst of this rapture.

"Rise then, since you are rising. You create me again. Ah! I have slandered you! Etc . . . Etc."

Change evil to good. Forced labor in Paradise.

Then finish up in an ambiguity highly disdainful, ironic and tonic at the same time; the verbal function, without any laudatory or pejorative coefficient: the obgame.

A Clearing in Winter

The blue born from gray, like pulp squeezed from a black raisin.

The whole atmosphere is like a teary eye, where the reasons and desire to rain have for the moment disappeared.

But everywhere the shower has left souvenirs that serve as mirrors to the beautiful day.

There is something tender in this union between two such different states of feeling. Something disarming in this gentle rain now ended.

Each puddle is like a butterfly wing under glass,
But it takes only a passing wheel to kick up the mud.

Mœurs nuptiales des chiens

Les mœurs nuptiales des chiens, c'est quelque chose! Dans un village de Bresse, en 1946... (je précise, car étant donné cette fameuse évolution des espèces, si elle se précipitait... ou s'il y avait mutation brusque: on ne sait jamais)...

Quel curieux ballet! Quelle tension!

C'est magnifique, ce mouvement qu'engendre la passion spécifique. Dramatique! Et comme ça a de belles courbes! Avec moments critiques, paroxystiques, et longue patience, persévérance immobile maniaque, ambages à très amples révolutions, circonvolutions, chasses, promenades à allure spéciale...

Oh! Et cette musique! Quelle variété!

Tous ces individus comme des spermatozoïdes, qui se rassemblent après d'invraisemblables, de ridicules détours.

Mais cette musique!

Cette femelle traquée; cruellement importunée; et ces mâles quêteurs, grondeurs, musiciens.

Cela dure des huit jours... (plus peut-être: je corrigerai quand ce sera fini).

Quels maniaques, ces chiens. Quel entêtement. Quelles sombres brutes. Quels grands bêtas! Tristes. Bornés. Quels emmerdeurs!

Ridicules d'entêtement. Plaintifs. L'air à l'écoute, au flair. Affairés. Afflairés. Haussant et fronçant tristement, comiquement les sourcils. Tout tendus: oreilles, reins, jarrets. Grondants. Plaintifs. Aveugles et sourds à toute autre chose qu'à leur détermination spécifique.

(Comparez cela à la grâce et à la violence des chats. A la grâce aussi des chevaux.)

Mais ce n'était pas ma chienne, c'était celle du voisin, le Facteur Féaux: je n'ai pas pu voir cela d'assez près, observer les organes de la dame, son odeur, ses traînées, ses pertes de semence.

The Nuptial Habits of Dogs

The nuptial habits of dogs are really something! In a village in Bresse, in 1946 . . . (I want to be precise because, considering this famous evolution of species, if it were to hasten . . . or if there were to be an unexpected mutation: one never knows) . . .

What a strange ballet! What tension!

This motion engendered by the specific passion is beautiful. Dramatic! And how lovely those curves! With critical moments, paroxystic, and drawn-out patience, perseverance of a maniacal immobility, circumlocutions in very slow revolutions, circumvolutions, pursuits, strolling in a special way.

Oh! And that music! What a variety!

All those individuals like spermatozooa, who come together after unbelievable, ridiculous detours.

But what music!

That hunted female; cruelly importuned; and those male hunters, grumblers, musicians.

This lasts a good week . . . (more perhaps: I'll correct it at the end).

What maniacs those dogs. What stubbornness. What heavy brutes. What chumps! Sad. Narrow-minded. What pains in the ass.

Ridiculously stubborn. Plaintive. Ears cocked, on the scent. Busy. Scenting. Raising and knitting their brows, sadly, comically. Everything strained: ears, backs, legs. Growling. Plaintive. Blind and dumb to everything else but their specific determination.

(Compare this to the grace and the violence of cats. To the grace of horses also.)

But it wasn't my bitch. It belonged to my neighbor, Féaux the postman: I was unable to look at it close enough, observe the organs of the lady, her smell, her movements, her losses of seed.

Je n'ai pu me rendre compte si elle avait commencé par être provocante, ou si seulement cela lui était venu (son état d'abord, ses pertes, son odeur, puis les mâles et leurs si longues, si importunes assiduités), si ça n'avait été pour elle qu'un étonnement douloureux et qu'une plainte, timide, avec déplacements mesurés, consentants.

Enfin, quel drame! Comme la vie, alors révélée, a dû lui paraître harassante, énervante, absurde!

Et la voilà blessée pour toujours,—moralement aussi! Mais elle aura ses beaux petits chiots... Pour elle seule, pendant quelque temps... Alors les mâles lui ficheront la paix, et quel bonheur avec ses petits, quel amusement même, quelle plénitude,—malgré parfois beaucoup d'encombrement entre les pattes et sous le ventre, beaucoup de fatigue.

Enfin, nous n'avons pas beaucoup dormi, pendant ces huit jours... Mais ça ne fait rien: on ne peut pas jouir de tout à la fois,—du sommeil et de quelque chose comme une série de représentations nocturnes au Théâtre Antique.

La lune par là-dessus (au-dessus des passions) m'a paru tenir aussi un grand rôle.

La Barque

La barque tire sur sa longe, hoche le corps d'un pied sur l'autre, inquiète et têtue comme un jeune cheval.

Ce n'est pourtant qu'un assez grossier réceptacle, une cuiller de bois sans manche: mais, creusée et cintrée pour permettre une direction du pilote, elle semble avoir son idée, comme une main faisant le signe couci-couça.

Montée, elle adopte une attitude passive, file doux, est facile à mener. Si elle se cabre, c'est pour les besoins de la cause.

Lâchée seule, elle suit le courant et va, comme tout au monde, à sa perte tel un fétu.

I was unable to determine if she had begun by being provocative, or if it had only come to her (her condition, her discharges, her smell, then the males and their attention, so long, so importunate), if it had only been a painful surprise for her, only a timid groan, with calculated and consenting movements.

What a sad story! How life, revealed to her at that moment, must have appeared harassing, bothersome, absurd!

And there she is, wounded for life,—morally also! But she will have her pretty little puppies . . . Alone to herself, for a little while . . . Then those males will leave her alone, and what joy with her little ones, even what fun, what fullness,—despite an occasional rough house between her paws and under her belly, and a lot of fatigue.

The fact is, we did not sleep much for a week . . . But that's of no importance: you can't always have everything,—sleep and something like a series of noctural performances at the Classic Theater.

The moon there above (above the passions) also seemed to me to have played an important part.

The Boat

The boat tugs on its line, moves its weight from one foot to the other, restless and stubborn like a young horse.

It is, however, only a crude receptacle, a wooden spoon without a handle: but, hollowed and curved to allow the pilot to guide it, it seems to have its own idea, like a hand making the sign.

Mounted, it adopts a passive attitude, moves gently, is easy to lead. If it rears, it is for the good of the cause.

Left alone, it follows the current and goes, like everything in the world; to its ruin like a straw.

La Gare

Il s'est formé depuis un siècle dans chaque ville ou bourg de quelque importance (et beaucoup de villages, de proche en proche, se sont trouvés atteints par contagion),

Un quartier phlegmoneux, sorte de plexus ou de nodosité tubéreuse, de ganglion pulsatile, d'oignon lacrymogène et charbonneux.

Gonflé de rires et de larmes, sali de fumées.

Un quartier matineux, où l'on ne se couche pas, où l'on passe les nuits.

Un quartier quelque peu infernal où l'on salit son linge et mouille ses mouchoirs.

Où chacun ne se rend qu'en des occasions précises, qui engagent tout l'homme, et même le plus souvent l'homme avec sa famille, ses hardes, ses bêtes, ses lares et tout son saint-frusquin.

Où les charrois de marchandises ailleurs plutôt cachés sont incessants, sur des pavés mal entretenus.

Où les hommes et les chevaux en long ne sont qu'à peine différenciés et mieux traités que les ballots, bagages et caisses de toutes sortes.

Comme le nœud d'une ganse où se nouent et dénouent, d'où partent et aboutissent des voies bizarres, à la fois raides et souples, et luisantes, où rien ne peut marcher, glisser, courir ou rouler sinon de longs, rapides et dangereux monstres tonnants et grinçants, parfois gémissants, hurlants ou sifflants, composés d'un matériel de carrosserie monstrueusement grossier, lourd et compliqué, et qui s'entourent de vapeurs et de fumées plus volumineuses par les jours froids, comme celles des naseaux des chevaux de poste.

Un lieu d'efforts maladroits et malheureux, où rien ne s'accomplit sans grosses difficultés de démarrage, manœuvre et parcours, sans bruits de forge ou de tonnerre, raclements, arrachements: rien d'aisé, de glissant, de propre, du moins tant que le réseau n'a pas été électrifié; où tremblent et à chaque instant menacent de s'écrouler en

The Station

During the last century, in every city and town of some importance (and in many villages close to one another, affected by the contagion),

A phlegmonious section has been built, a kind of plexus or tuberous nodosity, a pulsating ganglion, a lachrymonious and charcoaled onion.

Swollen by laughter and tears, dirtied by smoke.

A morning section, where no one goes to sleep, where nights are spent.

A somewhat infernal section where linen gets dirty, and handkerchiefs wet.

Where one only goes on special occasions, that completely take over a man, and even more often, man and family, his clothing, his beasts, his household gods, and the whole kit and caboodle.

Where the delivery trucks elsewhere kept out of sight appear everywhere on badly kept cobblestones.

Where on the whole it is hard to tell men from horses, or to see how they are treated better than packages, baggage, and crates of all types.

Like loops of braid that wind and unravel, from which strange strands come and go, both straight and curved, and shiny, where nothing can walk, slide, run or roll except those long, fast and dangerous monsters thundering and creaking, sometimes moaning, yelling or whistling, whose bodies are made of monstrously crude matter, heavy and complicated, surrounded by steam and smoke more voluminous on cold days, like you've seen coming out of the nostrils of relay horses.

A place of awkward and unhappy efforts, where nothing can be done without a great deal of trouble in getting started, maneuvering, clearing the track, without the noise of forge or thunder, scraping, tearing: nothing easy, smooth, clean at least as long as the line has not been electrified; where windows shake and at each

miettes les verrières, buffets à verrerie, lavabos à faïences ruisselantes et trous malodorants, petites voitures, châsses à sandwiches et garde-manger ambulants, lampisteries où se préparent, s'emmaillotent, se démaillotent, se mouchent et se torchent dans la crasse de chiffons graisseux les falots, les fanaux suintants, les lumignons, les clignotantes, les merveilleuses étoiles multicolores,—et jusqu'au bureau du chef de gare, cet irritable gamin:

C'est LA GARE, avec ses moustaches de chat.

Déclaration
Condition et destin de l'artiste

Les Fleurys, 14 *avril* 1950.

Novum organum.

I. Considérer l'artiste comme un chercheur (désireux, acharné, ravi) qui trouve parfois, un travailleur désintéressé.

(D'oû l'esthétique du tâtonnement, des redites, etc. (*Carnet du bois de pins*). Transcender le magma analogique et l'allégorie même. Parvenir à la formule claire. Sans trop de redites, sans trop d'explications.) Vertu de la recherche authentique donnée comme telle.

Qui trouve parfois, mais il ne s'intéresse pas à ses trouvailles comme telles: il continue à chercher.

Homme de laboratoire: laboratoire de l'expression. A partir 1° de la matière brute, des émotions qu'elle donne, du désir qu'elle inspire 2° de son moyen d'expression.

C'est un homme (entier) comme un autre.

Il ne *cherche* pas non plus à être *témoin*: il l'est.

Il éduque son moyen d'expression.

Exprime *face au monde* (à propos des émotions qu'il en reçoit) *son plus particulier*. Respecte son impression première: ce qu'il reçoit

instant are ready to fall into tiny pieces, glass doors, porcelain washstands dripping, and smelly holes, hand trucks, sandwich baskets, lunch wagons, lamp rooms where they prepare, diaper, undiaper, blow the noses, wipe with the filth of greasy rags, the lanterns, cracked signal lights, wicks, blinkers, the marvelous multicolored stars—and even the office of the station master, that irritable brat:

It's THE STATION, with its cat's whiskers.

Declaration
Condition and Destiny of the Artist

Les Fleurys, April 14, 1950

Novum organum.

I. To consider the artist as a researcher (anxious, stubborn, enraptured) who finds at times a disinterested worker.

(Hence the tentative esthetics, the repetitions, etc. (*Notebook of the Pine Forest*). To transcend the analogous magma, and even the allegory. To reach the clear formula. Without too many repetitions, without too many explanations.) The virtue of the authentic research taken as such.

Who finds at times, but who does not care for his discoveries as such: he continues to search.

Man of the laboratory: the laboratory of expression. Beginning first with brute matter, the emotions it gives, the desire it inspires, secondly with its means of expression.

He is a man (whole) like another.

Neither does he *seek* to be a *witness*: he is one.

He educates his means of expression.

Expresses *to the world* (concerning the emotions that he receives from it) *its utmost particularity*. Respects his first impressions:

des objets du monde. Cela doit compter plus que tout: pas d'autre vergogne. Il est là pour exprimer la nature muette (le mystère, le secret, à l'égal du savant).

Nouvelle conception de l'artiste, comme devant fournir des armes, des proverbes (proverbes du gratuit, de l'éternel) (Expression de Blin à propos d'Artaud: armes fulgurantes)

II. Cette idée de l'artiste est nouvelle.

Elle découle du progrès des sciences (théorie de la relativité), de la fonctionnarisation (Kafka), des nouvelles révolutions sociales (communisme, technocraties des nouvelles découvertes ethnologiques (civilisations nègres, primitives).

—du nouveau mythe de l'homme: de la notion de la relativité *humaine* (surréalisme, marxisme, freudisme). L'homme est un animal comme un autre. Sa fonction propre.

—de la mort de Dieu.

L'artiste résume la science, l'abolit, fait resurgir la vie, exprime le monde total.

Réjouit, récrée l'homme. Effet des catastrophes et bouleversements; guerres, atrocités, nouvelle barbarie.

*

Le nouvel humanisme: Philosophie des philosophies.
Psychologie de l'art.
Les Musées. Le goût de l'ancien.
L'abhumanisme de l'artiste.

*

Il ne peut être que révolutionnaire,
mais ne peut non plus que maintenir *les valeurs*.

Doit transcender les partis philosophiques et religieux (Rabelais, Montaigne, vers 1530,50: non protestants, non abattus par les troubles: souriant ou riant.)

those that he receives from objects in the world. That must count more than anything else: there must be no other scruples. He is there to express silent nature (the mystery, the secret, on a par with the scientist).

New conception of the artist, as the one who must provide weapons, proverbs (proverbs of gratuity, of the eternal) (Blin's expression about Artaud: flashing weapons)

II. This idea of the artist is new.

It stems from the progress of the sciences (theory of relativity), functionalization (Kafka), new social revolutions (Communism), the technocracy of the new ethnological discoveries (Negro civilizations, primitives),

—from the new myth of man: from the notion of *human* relativity (Surrealism, Marxism, Freudianism). Man is an animal like any other. His proper function.

—from the death of God.

The artist summarizes science, abolishes it, resuscitates life, expresses the complete world.

Rejoices, recreates man. Effect of catastrophes and upheavals; wars, atrocities, new barbarism.

*

The new humanism: Philosophy of philosophies.
Psychology of art.
Museums. The taste for the old.
The abhumanism of the artist.

*

He can only be a revolutionary,
but also can only maintain *values*.

Must transcend philosophic and religious parties (Rabelais, Montaigne, around 1530–50: not a Protestant, not saddened by the events: smiling or laughing.)

Une seule solution: exprimer la nature muette
en marquant son moyen d'expression,
le traitant sans vergogne (pour cela il faut en posséder les ressources)
Un certain gâtisme: naïveté retrouvée
repartir du balbutiement, du zéro.

*

Transcender classicisme et romantisme par le primat donné à la matière, à l'objet, aux qualités inouïes qui en sortent ce que Braque nomme le fortuit (ou le fatal?); par ce troisième terme: l'objet.

*

Ce que nous réclamons pour lui, pour cet ouvrier, ce chercheur: un nouveau Collège de France (rappeler les motifs de sa création par François Ier: laïcisation de la "recherche".)

A single solution: to express silent nature
by stressing its means of expression, treating it without shame (to do this one must possess all its resources)
A degree of senility: a naïveté rediscovered
to begin from stammerings, from zero.

*

To transcend classicism and romanticism by the primacy accorded to matter, to the object, to the unbelievable qualities that emerge from it
what Braque calls the fortuitous (or the fatal?); by this third term: the object.

*

What we demand for him, this worker, this researcher: a new Collège de France (recall the reasons for its creation by Francis I: the laicization of "research").

Jean Follain

Born 1903 in Canisy, Normandy

"Of course, if they had really wanted to restore the Place des Vosges to its former condition, they would have had to cut down the trees." Jean Follain looks out his window and sees one of the most beautiful squares in all of Paris. And he remembers its history as accurately as if he had been rewriting one of his very first books: the one on Paris. Follain, like an aged coat, leans over his book-filled desk. On all sides, books are asymmetrically piled up. Long ago the shelves were filled and now overflow with books of poems, anthologies, translations, and dictionaries (he has himself recently completed one on ecclesiastical terms). Follain sits in this hibernaculum, a man of the bench and of the desk, reflecting on contemporary issues with grace and noblesse oblige.

Jean Follain was the first poet I translated and the first with whom I had corresponded. I had struggled with those apparently easy poems for a summer, and since then, I had frequently revised them. Out of the corrections, readings that never ceased, I came to discover some of the secrets, some of the daring and some of the pleasures of this man who now answers my questions with precision and affability. As he speaks of Time I cannot avoid seeing a parallel between this theme and the Place des Vosges where the past is experienced without any emotional bric à brac. This square is not a museum; it is not a nostalgic moment, filled with reminiscences, but a place where people live in the ambiance of the past which they most often disregard. Only the poet from his window sees the effective meeting between the distant past when noblemen were encouraged to build their city homes here, and the weathered appearance of these same homes, long since transformed into apartments filled with ordinary people, and once in a while a poet.

Would you situate yourself in the poetic movement in France since the end of the war?

Your question is rather special and perhaps a difficult one to answer. To begin with, I cannot say that I began in 1945 since my first book

dates from 1933—the first one that really counts. I would also say that I was not oblivious to Surrealism though my poetry has been considered as a reaction against it. I do not believe the word "reaction" is too strong. Surrealist research did not greatly influence me, although Surrealism in itself has interested me enormously.

I strive to write a poetry that might be called—although the word does not say everything that should be said—a poetry of concentration that I would oppose to a type of poetry marked by its discursiveness, which has its value, and which should exist beside it. In this poetry of concentration there is a tightening of the text, a great value attributed to the poem itself, a sort of verbal incantation rather well controlled but which must maintain itself as an incantation.

There is in my work an obvious desire to apprehend the world and the object as well as men. I have been called the poet of the object—this has been frequently repeated. There is truth in that, but I wanted to go beyond this so-called objectivity, this poetic objectivity that has also been discussed in my work. It has often been said, and it is true, that I had a tendency of not using evident metaphors. There are, of course, a vast number of images in my work in the largest sense of the word, but there are perhaps no metaphors in the sense of comparison. In point of fact, metaphors are not my forte and I admire them greatly in other writers. I have even attempted at times to compose some myself, and I was satisfied with them in the beginning. But then I would say: "No! These metaphors do not go with my style." At the very most, there are hidden metaphors in my work. I do not exactly know the cause, but there is a desire on my part to bring things together in an unexpected manner in order to describe a particular sentiment, a particular vision of the world and to use the simplest words in order to give them back their virtue, their profound value.

There is in our language, as there is in all languages, a quantity of words that have been used up and to which it is necessary to give back a vitality: many words from our everyday language are to be considered in this manner. I have also been called by some the poet of the quotidian. But here again, I would not agree wholeheartedly, though there is a bit of truth in that appreciation. I have always had the tendency to show the value of the smallest gesture, but this human gesture is not necessarily a quotidian gesture; a tendency also of showing, of exteriorizing a type of poetry that I deeply feel: a poetry of duration, and also one that penetrates the mystery of time. Most of my titles hinge on time: *L'Usage du temps des jours*, *Tout instant*, *Des Heures*, etc. I have always been captivated by time, the sequence of time. And the more I think about my poems, the more I come to believe that I may have wanted to give importance to a poetry that would bring out the very existence of beings and of things. To name things, to make them exist in their very vibrancy, if one can say that, in their fleetingness, seems to me to be the object of poetry.

I have noticed in your poetry a frequent use of words that evoke the farm. That is, not only worn-out words, as you say, but also words that are no longer current today, perhaps even words of another time, even of another place since you now live in Paris and in an urban milieu. Is it nostalgia? Is it a Proustian quest? What is your intention when you speak of that time and of those places in your poems?

True, I want to speak about things of the past. However, though this may sound a bit paradoxical, when I speak of things of the past I do not want to speak about them in the tone of memories. The tone of memories or of regrets is not of my choosing. When I speak of the past, it is precisely to place it in the present, it is to give it back its life in the present, since the past has a contemporary life; it is to place it back into the present time, and in the general time, if you will, in absolute time.

As for the choice of words that you mentioned, there is no doubt that I have been influenced by words from my section of France, and not so much by words that are particular to where I come from, as by words that are French, though they are rarely used nowadays. These are very simple words. For example, there is a word that I am very fond of, a word that is no longer widely used: it is the word *cultivateur*. It's a French word, so that where I live it is still easily used. You see, these particular words please me, because there is something profoundly true in *cultivateur*. I mention this word specifically because I happened to think of it at the moment, but obviously, there would be many others that have the ring of truth for me. Take another example. There is a word *ondée* that is hardly ever used anymore, but which is a French word that means a heavy shower. I have heard that word ever since my childhood and it has a special vigor for me.

What determines whether your text is going to have the concise structure of a poem or whether it will become a prose poem?

I have always had the need (and you will find many examples of it in other writers) of wanting to express in prose what I had said in verse. I have often felt the need to use both forms to express the same theme, because each one brings something that the other does not. Prose has a different vision, that is evident, even though it operates on the same subject as does the poem, which also has its particular effect.

Do you feel a greater restraint when you write verse poems as opposed to prose poems, or is it only a question of a difference in thought?

What is expressed in verse is brought into sharper focus (*décanté*). But I also have need of a prose that is not as sharply defined. Verse serves to focus with greater clarity, to sublimate, it becomes, almost in a chemical sense, a sublimation of the vision.

PRINCIPAL WORKS: *Paris*, Ed. Corréa, 1935
Chants terrestres, Ed. Denoël, 1937
L'Epicerie d'enfance, Ed. Corréa, 1938
Ici-bas, Bruxelles, Journal des Poètes, série poétique, 88, 1941
Canisy, Gallimard, 1942
Inventaire, Ed. Debresse, 1942
Usage du temps, Nouvelle Revue Française, 1943
Exister, Gallimard, 1947
Chef-lieu, Gallimard, 1950
Les Choses données, Seghers, 1952
Territoires, Gallimard, 1953
Palais souterrain, Alès: P.A.B., 1953
Objets, Limoges: Rougerie, 1955
Tout instant, poèmes en prose, Gallimard, 1957
Des Heures, Gallimard, 1960
Poèmes et proses choisis, Gallimard, 1961
Appareil de la terre, Gallimard, 1964
D'Après tout, Gallimard, 1967

L'empailleur d'oiseaux

L'empailleur s'était assis
devant les gorges roses
les ailes vertes ou mauves
de ses passereaux
rêvant à son amante
au corps si différent
parfois si près aussi
de celui des oiseaux
qu'il lui paraissait
très étrange
dans ses courbes et ses volumes
dans ses couleurs et ses parures
et dans ses ombres.

Les passions

Un été passe
sur le monde
un chien a pour dix ans de vie
chacun poursuit sa passion
et si l'un boit du vin fort
l'autre refait la machine
propre à sa vengeance amère
ou dénude la poitrine
de la servante anonyme
tandis que frémit l'arbre
imperceptiblement.

The Taxidermist

The taxidermist sat
in front of the rose throats
the wings green or mauve
of his sparrows
dreaming of his love
her body so different
and yet at times so like
that of the birds
that it seemed to him
very strange
in its curves and its volumes
in its colors and its ornaments
and in its shadows.

The Passions

A summer passes
over the world
a dog has ten more years to live
each one pursues his passion
and if one drinks strong wine
the other fixes the machine
suited to his bitter vengeance
or bares the breasts
of the nameless servant
while the tree trembles
imperceptibly.

Écouter

Il y a ce qui rassure
et dort au creux de la chose
on l'écoute
dans la boucle du fleuve
dans la houille éclairant
de ses brasiers
le corps de la jeune fille
qui s'expose à la vie
dans la ramure et le jour clair
ou dans la nuit poignante.

La pomme rouge

Le Tintoret peignit sa fille morte
il passait des voitures au loin
le peintre est mort à son tour
de longs rails aujourd'hui
corsettent la terre
et la cisèlent
la Renaissance résiste
dans le clair-obscur des musées
les voix se muent
souvent même le silence
est comme épuisé
mais la pomme rouge demeure.

Listen

Some things reassure
and sleep at the heart of the matter
one hears it
in the bend of the river
in the white coals lighting
with their fire
the body of the young girl
who welcomes life
in the boughs and the clear day
or in the poignant night.

The Red Apple

Tintoretto painted his dead daughter
cars are passing in the distance
the painter died in his turn
long rails today
corset the earth
and chisel it
the Renaissance resists
in the chiaroscuro of museums
the voices change
often even the silence
is almost exhausted
but the red apple remains.

Instant

Tant de visages sont
aux tournants
d'une lente existence
près des mêmes vitres
accueillantes au soleil.
C'est quand passe l'homme
sa poitrine solide, ses jambes alourdies
son sourire
que vibre le mieux
l'instant pur
du seul épi de blé
que sa main insoucieuse cueille
le faisant échapper à la faux.

Le Feu

De grands lierres s'étiraient
sur la maison grise
du métaphysicien
le feu y prit une nuit
éclairant la plaine rase
dans l'air flottèrent les cendres
dans l'odeur du foin brûlé
puis les cieux passèrent calmés
sur la ruine assaillie
par beaucoup d'enfants sans mère
qui sur ses brèches jouèrent
vêtus de haillons noircis
imaginant leur vie longue.

Instant

So many faces are
at the turnings
of a slow existence
near the same windows
welcoming the sun.
It is when a man passes
his chest solid, his legs sturdy
his smile
that pulses stronger
the pure moment
of the single spear of wheat
which his careless hand picks
letting it escape the scythe.

Fire

Tall ivy stretched over
the weathered house
of the metaphysician
one night it caught fire
in the air ashes floated
in the smell of burned hay
then clouds passed becalmed
over the ruin assaulted
by many orphans
who played in its breaches
dressed in black rags
imagining their future.

Accords

C'est la main dans la main
que doucement se sourient
deux frères en rébellion
il se traîne un fin nuage
sur le faubourg ocreux
aux fenêtres carrées
découpées dans ses murs
des visages regardent
s'aider des enfants graves
pour passer le ruisseau;
s'appuyant à l'arbre
sans feuilles et sans fruits
un prévoyant médite
sur le bord d'un abîme.

Artisans

Les artisans pleins d'ordre
savent combler l'heure
qui s'évanouit sous leurs doigts
tel refait inlassable
le cercle et l'hexagone
dans le soir libéral;
l'autre a fini de noircir les harnais
son enfant s'endort
dans le berceau à l'osier sec;
le plus habile
croit fatiguer la mort au mieux
laisse s'étendre les ombres
sur la place des fêtes
sans forcer les songes.

Agreements

Hand in hand
two brothers in rebellion
tenderly smile at each other
a thin cloud drags itself
over the ocherous suburb
at the square windows
cut out of its walls
faces are watching
solemn children help each other
across the stream;
leaning against a tree
without leaves or fruit
a cautious man meditates
on the edge of an abyss.

Artisans

Orderly workmen
know how to fill the hour
that slips through their fingers
one untiringly recreates
the circle and the hexagon
in the generous evening;
the other has finished blackening the harness
his child falls asleep
in a dry wicker cradle;
the cleverest one
thinks he can weary death at best
allows shadows to fall
on the village square
without chancing dreams.

Boutique

Des hommes viennent chercher
avec un lent sourire
des paquets clos
parfois une bougie blanche
dans cette boutique austère
où pendent les sabots ornés
leur voix clame:
«Y a-t-il du monde?»
Une femme vient enfin
les servir de ses mains
ayant cueilli l'herbe
au bord de ces chemins
que traverse si vite un lièvre
d'espèce commune.

Époques

Que de main-d'œuvre
dans ces tressaillants rideaux
figurant des dieux
certains bourgeois acclamèrent
d'autres se terrèrent
entre des murs nus
un corps parfois s'offre
dans ces époques troublées
s'il y survit
il se peut qu'il ouvre la porte
donnant sur une cour glacée
où gît un mannequin
aux yeux bleus
couvert de terre argileuse.

Shop

Men come to get
with a slow smile
wrapped packages
sometimes a white candle
in this austere shop
where ornate wooden shoes hang
their voices ring out:
"Anybody here?"
A woman comes at last
to serve them with her hands
having gathered the grass
at the edge of these paths
so rapidly crossed by a hare
of the common sort.

Epochs

So much workmanship
in these trembling curtains
depicting the gods
some good men applauded
others went to earth
between the bare walls
sometimes a shape appears
in these troubled epochs
if he survives them
he may open the door
on a frozen courtyard
where a mannikin lies
its blue eyes
covered with clay.

Guillevic

Born 1907 in Carnac, Brittany

History embeds itself in the walls of Paris streets. Each one has a public life, posters and graffiti, and a past, a plain mark on a house, a date, the name of a man, the death of another. The walls, like guardians, watch over the passing of tenants, stores, and the movement of traffic, the only indications that the street is not absolutely self-contained. The street has recognizable privileges, obscurities and obstacles that are both evident and secret. Like a landscape, the street organically absorbs the changes that have been introduced. It perpetuates itself: indivisible. It does not tolerate profound modifications on its outward nature: rather, trusting to the coloration of time, it succeeds in reestablishing the particular harmony that formerly reigned.

Nothing on this street is exceptional. It resembles adjacent streets. It has a few stores, a ceramic shop recessed off the sidewalk and protected by an iron gate. On the right side, on the corner, there is a bookshop. Further down, there is a white-washed house.

When you look down rue Grégoire de Tours from the boulevard Saint-Germain, it is the narrowness that imposes itself and the small white-washed house on the right, inside the curb. The brilliance of the color is reminiscent of a Mediterranean village. Yet even here the white is acceptable. It too will soon shed its novelty and blend with its neighbors. Up the winding, narrow staircase. When the bell rings, Guillevic answers. He stands like one of those monolithic stones of Carnac, filled with invisible knowledge and power, sensitive to dimensions, to the quality of words, to the stems that link one to the other. But the immobility of that rocky coast is less attuned to the revelatory chords that vibrate objects and peoples. Like all poets, he lives peripherally, gaining from that advantage a special gift of observation, a point of reflection. He is both rock and vibration, emitting and blocking, perfecting his voice. In his simply furnished apartment, to which he has retired after years of service as a high government civil servant in the Ministry of Finance, Guillevic lives now quietly, traveling, tasting a measure of fame. But the sale of poetry is slow! He speaks without rancor about the belated recognition that has fallen upon his massive shoulders. And now, walking toward Gallimard, Guillevic continues to discuss the present state of French poetry. He is happy that translations of his work have made him known in Eastern Europe. In the United States there have also been a few translations prior to those included in this volume. But still he waits, good-humoredly, for a larger and more representative collection. If poetry now occupies his time, critics also loom large on the horizon. Guillevic, like other poets to whom I spoke, bewailed the quality of French critics. There are practically none in the daily press and very few in the literary reviews. His latest collection, filled with a delicate irony, failed to please the critics who would have preferred a repetition of his earlier success with Carnac. *Fortunately, Guillevic, like his friend André Frénaud, does not depend on others: anchored firmly within his imagination, objects that determine reality create anew the relationships between the poet and the world in a state of contentment.*

Would you briefly indicate where you would place yourself in the post-1945 poetic movement?

I have sometimes been classified with the materialist poets. I have also been classified with the politically oriented poets. I don't believe that says much. Undoubtedly, it is difficult for a poet to situate himself, because in order to do so, it is first necessary to know the totality of the situation. I don't know if that is exactly my case. Next, it is necessary to know oneself quite well, and further, know one's narcissism, which may again not be the case for me. So that I will try to answer the question in good faith but without any guarantees.

I believe that I belong to a generation. A generation that has not made much noise, which has not waved any flags, which has not written shattering manifestos. It is a generation of men born around 1905—that is, a generation that includes such poets as Char. Though Char, born in 1907, straddles my generation and that of the Surrealists, from many points of view he is of our generation. Others are Follain, Tardieu, and Frénaud. I believe that we have in common certain traits that are not easily defined, that one could first try to define by saying that we were to a degree in opposition to Surrealism, first of all because of certain external circumstantial reasons. Surrealism was a Parisian movement, an urban movement, and we were all from the provinces, some of us were even peasants. Surrealism touched men younger than us, because it came to them after having been diluted. But in my own case, in 1925, or in 1930, when I was twenty-three years old and living in Alsace, I had no means of buying books, so I ignored a great many things. Alright. That is a sort of circumstantial or anecdotal reason. And then, the fact is, our generation was . . . I should have mentioned one of the most important poets, Pierre Seghers . . . we were not Surrealists because . . . we were . . . I dare not use the word because it has been dishonored and has become irritating: it is the word realist. I prefer poets, not realists perhaps, but poets that interest us in the real, the real that we confront every day. A type of poetry that one might call of the tragic quotidian; not an intimate poetry, but a poetry of the daily tragic experience. And although I hate to use the word (it must be used at times), we refused what I may be allowed to call "escape" (*fuite*) into an invented surreality. We accepted life in its reality, and the struggle with reality, in order to live, to live better. I forgot to mention Ponge, for example, but that goes without saying, one often forgets the most important individuals. . . . One can oppose Ponge to Frénaud; Frénaud, whom I kid at times when I call him Alfred de Vigny, has a romantic side, which Ponge does not. But there is between them a common interest, a desire to write a poetry of the actual world, and I think that I belong to this generation, with certain reservations, and these are due to something that I cannot be precise about. Is it because I come from Brittany? I will not go and seek astrological explanations, I don't believe in them, but still . . . an individual is an individual. I do have in this particular generation a formal distinction, although Follain is not far from me on this score: that is, I write brief poems. Why? I have practiced the art of the concise, of the elliptical expression because I needed it. This style was given to me, in a large measure, by dreams. I dreamed for a long while, for years. Then I wrote poems that were very different, but when I dreamed, I saw short poems, inscribed on trees; and the dream ended when I began to write short poems, poems that are called lapidary. That is about where I stand, to answer the first question.

Would you discuss the way in which you compose your poems? How do you work? I know, for example, that your vocabulary is quite different from that of other poets writing today.

That's an interesting question, and it's a question that was once asked of me. A student said to me: "Sir, why is your vocabulary so poor?" That's a very interesting question. I had never thought about it. I may have barely been conscious of it. First of all, there is that strange thing: I have always lived in France, at least until my twentieth year, but in sections of the country where French was not spoken around me. French was only spoken in my family. Either Walloon was spoken, or Breton or Alsatian. The vocabulary that I had in French was consequently either what I heard at home or what I heard in school: that is, a limited vocabulary. And I came from a very poor family. There were no books at home. My parents did not read. I was not like Sartre. I would be unable to write *Les Mots*. Words to me were those of utility, the language of everyday. That's the only French I ever learned. I lived in a non-cultured environment; you might say that even the school world was not cultivated. This explains my limited vocabulary.

Now, as to my way of composing . . . well, the poem comes to me when it comes. Valéry once said that the first line is given to us. That is sometimes correct. Not frequently in my case. Something is given, something which is a provocation, an opening. It is as if a curtain were lifted, or a wall broken down. I enter into contact with something. What is given to me is a coloration, a tonality, yes, a feeling for a thing. Then I begin. But I don't go very far. In general, I go without knowing where I'm going. I try to circumscribe a poetic thought, not the philosophic thought which hides behind this thing with which I have come into contact. And then with words, if I dare express myself in this manner, words for me are both the quarry and the pickaxe. I search in words and with words. I search for what is concealed behind what I have found, and I write without bothering about whether it is good or not, if it is correct, if it is beautiful, if it is French. I write. It is not automatic writing because my critical sense still intervenes. I seek out every part, and every part of my being intervenes. And then, I work a lot, I start over and over again. I remember what Braque once said: "The painting is on the other side of the canvas." Well, the poem is also on the other side of something, perhaps not behind the piece of paper, but it has to be located. It is necessary to dig and simultaneously to fish for it: well, you've got to find it. It isn't that I believe in inspiration, it isn't that I believe in some sort of predestination, but as Rimbaud said: "I is another." Isn't that so? The work consequently is not a confession, it is not an intimate diary. It is a question of finding something. The poet is the person who, I believe, has the singular gift of finding that particular thing. Why? Because he is at once both attuned to the interior and to the exterior world as well as to language. And I think he writes because he is particularly sensitive to the world and also sensitive to language. I guess that is his gift, his task.

PRINCIPAL WORKS: *Requiem*, Tschamm, 1938
Terraqué, Gallimard, 1942
Amulettes, Seghers, 1946
Exécutoire, Gallimard, 1947
Fractures, Ed. de Minuit, 1947
Les Chansons d'Antonin Blond, Seghers, 1949
Gagner, Gallimard, 1949
Envie de vivre, Seghers, 1951
Terre à bonheur, Seghers, 1953
Trente et un Sonnets, Gallimard, 1954
Carnac, Gallimard, 1961
Sphères, Gallimard, 1963
Euclidiennes, Gallimard, 1967

Il tremblait devant la lumière
Et tremblait devant les rameaux.

Il n'était pas content des fenêtres
Et se méfiait des oiseaux.

Il n'avait pu
Être davantage.

Je n'ai jamais compris
Pourquoi, où qu'ils soient,
Toujours les gens causaient

Et rarement
j'ai su de quoi.

Tu fais comme eux,
Tu veux causer,
Tu te racontes.

Ils ont dit oui
A la pourriture.

Ils ont accepté,
Ils nous ont quittés.

Nous n'avons rien à voir
Avec leur pourriture.

He trembled in front of the light
And trembled in front of the branches.

He found no joy in the windows
And was wary of birds.

More
He could not have been.

I have never understood
Why, wherever they were
People always chattered

And I rarely knew
What it was all about.

You do what they do,
You want to chatter,
You go on about yourself.

They said yes
To filth.

They accepted,
They left us.

We have nothing to do
With their filth.

Il y aura toujours dans l'automne
Une pomme sur le point de tomber.

Il y aura toujours dans l'hiver
Une fontaine sur le point de geler.

Que les corbeaux
S'enfuient de peur à notre approche,
C'est leur droit. Nous pouvons aller.

De l'espoir il y en aura
Sur les rameaux.

Et puis, nous ne sommes pas malades
De la terre.

L'ennemi,
Nous le connaissons.

Encore une fois,
Que faire avec toi,
Nous qui pouvons?

Debout au soleil,
Fiers de nos travaux,
Toujours approchant d'un plus grand secret

Et toi un remords
A n'en pas finir.

In autumn there will always be
An apple ready to fall.

In winter there will always be
A fountain ready to freeze.

Let the frightened crows
Flee in fear at our approach
It's their right. We can go on.

There will be hope
On the branches.

And anyway, we are not sick
Of the earth.

The enemy,
We know him.

Once again,
What to do with you,
We who are able?

Standing in the sun,
Proud of our labors,
Always nearing a greater secret

And you
A never ending remorse.

L'école publique

A Saint-Jean-Brévelay notre école publique
Était petite et très, très pauvre : des carreaux
Manquaient et pour finir c'est qu'il en manquait trop
Pour qu'on mette partout du carton par applique,

Car il faut voir bien clair lorsque le maître explique.
Alors le vent soufflait par tous ces soupiraux
Et nous avons eu froid souvent sous nos sarraux.
Par surcroît le plancher était épisodique

Et l'on sait qu'avec l'eau du toit la terre fait
Des espèces de lacs boueux d'un bel effet.
—Pourtant j'ai bien appris dans cette pauvre école :

Orthographe, calcul, histoire des Français,
Le quatorze juillet, Valmy, la Carmagnole,
Le progrès, ses reculs, et, toujours, son succès.

Tu viens et tu vas
Mais dans des limites

Fixées par une loi
Qui n'est pas de toi.

Nous avons en commun
L'expérience du mur.

Public School

Our public school in Saint-Jean Brévelay
Was small and very very poor: there were
Few panes, and soon too many were missing
For us to put cardboard in all of them,

Because you have to see clearly when the teacher explains.
Then the wind blew in through all those vents
And we were often cold in our overalls.
And besides that, the floors were irregular

And as you know with the water from the roof the ground
Makes a beautiful kind of muddy lake.
—Still I learned a lot in that poor school:

Spelling, arithmetic, French history,
The fourteenth of July, Valmy, the Carmagnole,
Progress, its recessions, and always, its success.

You come and you go
But within limits

Fixed by a law
Which is not yours.

We have in common
The experience of the wall.

Exposé
(*Fragments*)

I

Que déjà je me lève en ce matin d'été
Sans regretter longtemps la nuit et le repos,

Que déjà je me lève
Et que j'aie cette envie d'eau froide
Pour ma nuque et pour mon visage,

Que je regarde avec envie
L'abeille en grand travail
Et que je la comprenne,

Que déjà je me lève et voie le buis,
Qui probablement travaille autant que l'abeille,
Et que j'en sois content,

Que je me sois levé au-devant de la lumière
Et que je sache: la journée est à ouvrir,

Déjà, c'est victoire.

Tous les paysages
Qu'il a fallu voir.

Tous les paysages
Où tu n'étais pas

Et qui t'accusaient
De n'y être pas.

Exposé
(*Fragments*)

I

If I am already out of bed this summer morning
Without long regretting the end of night and rest,

If I can already be up
And have such a desire for cold water
On my neck and face,

If I can look with envy
At the bee busily at work
And understand it,

If I can already get up and see the boxwood tree
That probably works as much as the bee,
And be happy about it,

If I can be up before the light
And know: the day is about to break,

Then that is already a victory.

All the landscapes
That had to be seen.

All the landscapes
Where you were not

And which accused you
Of not being there.

Souvenir

A la mémoire de Gabriel Péri

Ce n'est pas vrai qu'un mort
Soit comme un vague empire
Plein d'ordres et de bruit,

Qu'il nous envie
Quand nous mangeons.

Ce n'est pas vrai qu'un mort
Soit du sang ou du lait la nuit plus haut que nous.

Ce n'est pas lui qui rit dans l'arbre et dans le vent
Si l'on pleure au village.

Ce n'est pas lui non plus
Qui fait tomber les bols quand on tourne le dos
Ou la suie sur le feu.

Ce n'est jamais un mort
Qui nous prend à parti dans les yeux des chevreaux.

Il ne faut pas mentir,
Rien n'est si mort qu'un mort.

—Mais c'est vrai que des morts
Font sur terre un silence
Plus fort que le sommeil.

Souvenir

In memory of Gabriel Péri

It is not true that a dead man
Is like a vague empire
Full of orders and noise,

That he envies us
When we eat.

It is not true that a dead man
Should be more of blood or milk at night than we.

He is not the one who laughs in the tree and in the wind
If one cries in the village.

Neither is he the one
Who knocks down the bowls when our backs are turned
Or the soot in the fire.

It is never a dead man
Who takes us to task in the eyes of goats.

There is no use lying,
Nothing is as dead as a dead man.

—But it is true that some dead
On earth make a silence
Louder than sleep.

André Frénaud

Born 1907 in Montceau-les-Mines, Burgundy

He would not write a poem about New York, nor would he have his characters follow its straight lines. Still, there are so many elements with which to work that it would be impossible for this poet to be insensitive to them.

"Where shall we go?" André Frénaud asks. We are on Madison Avenue, going toward 34th Street in search of a piece of luggage and perhaps a wash-and-wear shirt. This is his first visit to the United States and, more than any visitor I have ever accompanied, André Frénaud reacts to every skyward movement that meets his gaze. An ebullient man, full of a Burgundian love of life, a material feeling for observable reality, a direct contact with people especially here where he speaks no English.

We walk. "I am only a poet at times." And yet at every instant he sees a shape, a color, a cloud, sun and windows, buildings and a special density to the streets. As we push our way against the crowd, carrying a newly purchased valise, André Frénaud marvels at the proportions and the shadows, investing the city with no other mystery but its own nature, revealed to itself in a glance. Frénaud is indefatigable. He maintains a rhythm of observation that creates its own criteria and its own mood. Things are classified; they are retained.

André Frénaud promises to learn English before his next visit. In the meantime, we sit, perched on high stools in a bar around the corner from the Chelsea Hotel where he is staying. His pleasure at being in New York, drinking Miller's High Life, seeing, tasting this world, is a contagious one. As he has traveled in Europe (teaching one year at the University in Lwów in Poland), so the theme of the voyage has had a coherence in his poems that has managed to transmute itself into another symbolic domain into which we cross by way of his invention. Guardian and sybil, the poet knows and does not know, but in his constitution, he has incorporated, frequently without intention, the markings of a secret path. This affection that André Frénaud has for the peasant and the worker, for man as a particular being, is thus not a conception worked out in the laboratory of his mind. It is his character, full of outward force and movement, ready to benefit and love, to admire and to judge the beauty in people as well as in the experiences that they have shared with him. The real world will first be discovered. Later, there will be time for the others.

Where would you place yourself, especially in relationship to the evolution of French poetry since the end of the war? How would you consider your position from an esthetic point of view? From a thematic one?

I have, I would say, a particularity: I began writing poems very late, though I had jotted down a few poems when I was fifteen or sixteen. I didn't keep any of them because they weren't any good and I then had very different literary ambitions. At that time, I was most interested in pursuing a career in social psychology. I studied philosophy, and only began my second blossoming quite late, in 1938, at the age of thirty-one, which is absolutely exceptional, and must be attributed most probably to a sort of paralysis or inhibition.

In any case, one fine day in 1938, in April 1938, a strange phenomenon occurred which constituted itself in my mouth under my tongue: a text, and this text which I didn't really know how to interpret, was taking shape not so much through visual images as through a realization of words, words that were in open conflict with each other, that were confused, that were changing, becoming other words until a little object had finally taken shape, sufficiently formed for me to go up to my friends who were sitting around at a cafe near the Porte Saint Denis and say to them: "I think I've written a poem!" And I said to them: *Epitaphe*, because my first poem, the one that was my point of departure, the birth of my poetry was an epitaph. As you can see, my poetry was late in coming, though at times my friends used to say: "You're a poet" and I would reply: "You're wrong, I am not a poet." But I guess I was one, even if I developed my vocation late in life, as the clerics would say.

And then, you might add that I am just like the people of my generation, the inheritor of poets who preceded me. The generation that immediately preceded mine was the prestigious Surrealist generation. I only got to know them after I had returned from captivity in 1942, and then I became friends first with Eluard and then with Queneau, Leiris, Prévert, Char, all of whom became my friends. I had not personally known this generation of Surrealists before the war, but it had made an impression on me. Since that time, I have become more and more critical of Surrealism, all the while recognizing its merit.

What I am trying to say is that, contrary to what is too often believed in America, and not only in America but also in France, the great innovator in French poetry is not Breton and his friends, but Baudelaire, Rimbaud, Mallarmé, Lautréamont, and Jarry, who appear to me to be more unilateral. I think that it is a result of the works of these geniuses that there has occurred a revolutionary dialectic in French poetry, carried through Apollinaire and Reverdy, so that the Surrealists must be seen as an extreme development.

Given this perspective, I should place myself probably in the camp of those who do not consider the Surrealists as representing something exorbitant that has radically broken with the past. They were young men, very appealing and ardent. In the breakdown after the war of 1914–18, and later under the impact of DADA, they argued, full of emotion, irrationality and folly. However, they seem to me, twenty-five or thirty years later, to fit into the revolution of French poetry begun by Baudelaire and Rimbaud.

Thus, I belong to that generation which reacted to French poetry, which reacted to Surrealism, with it and against it, in a movement that sought to deepen that poetry which had engendered Baudelaire, Rimbaud, Jarry.

You have just spoken about this involvement with folly as being characteristic of the Surrealists. It seems to me there is an involvement with reality in your own work that is quite different. For example, you have strongly attached yourself to the places of your youth, to the places you have visited and which you have succeeded in transforming. Starting out from an extremely concrete basis, you have described a voyage that wends its way to a much more philosophic region, a much more humanistic one, than what was apparently occurring in the contemporary Surrealist texts.

I understand what you mean. I begin with reality, I deepen it, I would take that reality as a point of departure, a basic questioning that I would then attempt to follow. A sort of a quest. Whereas the Surrealists, turning their backs on reality, from the very beginning sought out a surreality. What happens in my poem? You say that I speak about the places of my childhood, of the reality that I experienced, that this is the beginning, that it is from a particular place, frequently, at a particular moment, with which the poet identifies, with which he finds himself in contact, in agreement, that the poem begins. But then the poet immediately goes deeper, wider, more into the interior, and it is with that place that he feels an unknown and marvelous agreement, rare, where he shuts himself out as such, as a man, with his usual means of coming into contact with the world. It is then that he is given other means of access, it is in that shock situation that the poet shapes things as he moves hesitatingly about.

True, I have a certain background in philosophy, but it isn't so much a question of background. There is in my work a type of questioning concerning the problem of being and the pursuit of that Man that we are. I am speaking here less of my explicit intentions than I am of the way my work has been interpreted by critics who have thought my work revealed a pursuit of man himself, and what he sought, in an effort to go beyond his condition, his contradictions, to go beyond his misery, to arrive at a state of joy, to arrive there through Yin and Yang, to the Tao, but this is a difficult thing to explain . . .

Isn't there a deeply tragic concern when you say that you must seek happiness through a dialectical confrontation that brings all the tensions, whether verbal or thematic, to a sort of resolution, a sort of synthesis which can be harmonious with your will, but which, by definition, cannot be found, and whose function it is to provoke in your work a type of perpetual movement? As one goes from poem to poem, from theme to theme, one has the feeling of traveling, of a philosophic voyage, of a voyage that is particularly tragic, since although formed out of familiar faces and cities that have made an impression on you, these things finally never have been able to offer you a satisfactory answer. The work, it seems, has been more successful than the goal, which has remained inaccessible. And even when reached, it has been insufficient.

You're absolutely right. There is no paradise, and that is, as you know, the title of one of my books. It is quite evident that the poet, like any man, is unsatisfied when he finds himself in that state of misery which is the fate of all men, for whom action is not the sister of dream, as Baudelaire remarked. The poet, it appears, is the one who seeks out a means of communication, and since he has a vocation that allows him access to man and a means of going beyond the usual means of knowledge, it may happen that he will undergo an experience where he is annihilated as himself and opens out onto totality—where he becomes the spokesman for that which exists and for man himself. "The Shepherd of Being" as Heidegger so rightly called the poet. And it is true that he cannot stop anywhere, that there are only paths reaching out, and that the poet is like Everyman burdened by limitations, death, contradictions without remedy. And yet he isolates from a certain type of experience little objects that mediate for an instant the overreaching element of communication in the Baudelairian sense.

One last question. We have been discussing themes, but there is another aspect to your work, and it is the question of language. Doesn't language itself pose certain problems similar to those asked elsewhere in the quest for the infinite? That is, how do you come to be satisfied by the very words that you use? How would you describe the combat that exists in this profusion of words at your disposal? I know that you enjoy mixing styles, cutting, making us aware that there are times when the reader must recognize your presence, so that instead of a continuous lyrical line, interruptions occur, plays of words. Would you agree that all this is done to make us take notice that it is not just a matter of themes, but that there is also a tension which is purely verbal at your disposition, and that these very words also present you with an act of defiance similar to the subject you are seeking?

The subject or the object that I seek, I do not seek after it in any other way but through language. Most of the time I am a non-poet, yet at times something extraordinary occurs, and that extraordinary something means that words begin to speak. It is like a revolution of language, and the poet does not necessarily know what is happening. When you say that I am seeking out something, that I attempt to reach a synthesis, it is a manner of speaking that I have used myself, but actually it isn't so much a question of preconceived intentions, or desire, neither is there a specific subject that is being sought out. There is an irruption of words, as I have called one of my poems, a movement, something which takes hold of the poet, and words begin . . . What is the meaning of it all? The poet does not know. I remember, for example, about the poem *Epitaphe*, that when I had finished it, I saw that it did not lack meaning, but I hesitated on a number of possible meanings. I do not now want to explicate the poem, but there are multiple explanations that offer themselves when I read the poem on succeeding occasions that are opposed to previous explanations, and that demonstrate that the poem has not yet been exhausted of its meaning. The poem has gone beyond the poet. He has composed an ambiguous object, multivalent, and infinitely richer in sense then he suspected and sought to imply.

There is a sort of logic in the succession of words themselves . . .

There is a revelation through language of subterranean depths, of the self, which is not the self, which is that part of the self which is unavowed, forbidden, pushed back, the I . . . but through the revelation of that subterranean murmur which symbolically represents conflicts without remedies and that begins to operate through poetry, there occurs an opening onto the being and a revelation of that state which is the poet's vocation: to become, as Heidegger noted, the "Shepherd of Being."

PRINCIPAL WORKS: *Les Rois mages*, Seghers, 1943
Soleil irréductible, Neuchâtel-Paris, Ides et Calendes, 1946
La Noce noire, Seghers, 1947
La Femme de ma vie, A. Blaizot, 1947
Poèmes de Brandebourg, Gallimard, 1948
Poèmes de dessous le plancher, Gallimard, 1949
Les Paysans, Jean Aubier, 1951
Source entière, Seghers, 1953
Passage de la visitation, G.L.M., 1956
Excrétions, misères et facéties (S. Sciascia), Caltanissetta, Rome, 1959
Agonie du Général Krivitski, P. J. Oswald, 1960
Pour l'office des morts, Alès, P.A.B., 1961
Il n'y a pas de paradis, poèmes, Gallimard, 1962 (ed. Coll. de Poésie, 1967)
L'étape dans la clairière, Gallimard, 1966
La Sainte Face, Gallimard, 1968

Il n'y a pas de paradis

à Dylan Thomas

Je ne peux entendre la musique de l'être
Je n'ai reçu le pouvoir de l'imaginer
Mon amour s'alimente à un non-amour
Je n'avance qu'attisé par son refus
Il m'emporte dans ses grands bras de rien
Son silence me sépare de ma vie

Être sereinement brûlant que j'assiège
quand enfin je vais l'atteindre dans les yeux
sa flamme a déjà creusé les miens m'a fait cendres
Qu'importe après le murmure misérable du poème
C'est néant cela non le paradis.

Je venais d'apprendre par une personne amie de Dylan Thomas qu'au cours d'une conversation celui-ci, imaginant et rêvant, s'était écrié: «Je voudrais faire entendre la musique du Paradis.»

Pays retrouvé

Mon cœur moins désaccordé de tout ce qu'il aimait
je ne fais plus obstacle à ce pays bien-aimé
J'ai dépassé ma fureur j'ai découvert
le passé accueillant Aujourd'hui je peux j'ose

Je me fie au chemin j'épèle ici sans crainte
la montée les détours Un songe vrai s'étale
Je m'y retrouve dans le murmure qui ne cesse pas
Le vent rien que le vent me mène où je désire

There is No Paradise

for Dylan Thomas

I cannot hear the music of existence
I have not been given the power to imagine it
My love feeds on non-love
I cannot move unless stirred by its refusal
It carries me away in its huge arms of nothing
Its silence separates me from my life

Being serenely burning that I besiege
when finally I have reached its eyes
its flame has already hollowed mine made me ashes
What matters after the poor murmur of the poem
Is nothingness—not paradise.

Home Again

My heart less out of tune with all that it loved
I no longer reject my beloved country
I have gone beyond my anger I have discovered
the welcoming past Today I can I dare

I trust myself to the path I spell out here without fear
the rise the detours One true dream emerges
and here I find myself again in the ceaseless murmur
The wind nothing but the wind takes me where I want to go

Des paroles inconnues me parviennent familières
Des regards bienveillants me suivent dans les arbres
Je me reconnais ici j'avoue mon pays cette terre-ci
et toute contrée où des hameaux apparaissent
où des coqs flambent près de la tour
avec la verveine dans le potager les massifs entre les murs

Les rangées des vignes se tiennent sur les versants
et les nuages se promènent lentement dans l'azur
creusant d'ombre la plaine où les céréales jaunissent
Tout est beau qui s'entrouvre aujourd'hui où je passe
O je me souviendrai de ce vrai pain des hommes
Je veux goûter de ces raisins qui sèchent
pendus sous la galerie.

9–10 février 1957

Haineusement mon amour la poésie

Comme un serpent qui remonte les rivières
comme une épée qui tombe reparaît sans mot dire
comme une grosse femme qui bout
comme une paire de haricots qui débouche
par-dessus la terre râtissée
comme sur un mur qu'éboule l'ardeur de la salamandre
seul feu elle traverse étincelante le vide
comme le temps travaillé par la nuit
obscure comme un ver luisant
branchue comme une étoile longuement éteinte
qui tout à coup reprend lumière
haineusement mon amour la poésie.

6 avril 1945

With unknown words I find myself familiar
Kind looks follow me among the trees
I recognize myself here I accept my country this very earth
and the whole land where towns spring up
where cocks flame near the tower
with verbena in the garden, hedges between the walls

The rows of vines stand on the slopes
And the clouds slowly wander in the sky
deepening with shade the plain where the grain is ripening
Today where I walk all things that open are beautiful
O I will remember this true bread of mankind
I want to taste those drying grapes
hanging under the balcony.

Hatefully Poetry My Love

Like a serpent that ascends the rivers
like a sword that fallen reappears without a word
like a fat woman that boils over
like a pair of stringbeans that appear
above the raked earth
like a wall that crumbles under the heat of the salamander
casting sparks into the void when it crosses fire
like time worked over by night
obscure like a firefly
branched like a long extinguished star
that suddenly lights up again
hatefully poetry my love.

Machine inutile

Une machine à faire du bruit
qui s'ébroue et supplie et proclame
pas seulement pour vous faire taire
peut-être pas pour m'amuser
construite en mots dépaysés
pour se décolorer l'un par l'autre
pour entrer dans l'épais du grain
pour y trouer tous les grains
pour y passer par les trous
pour y pomper l'eau imprenable
dont le courant gronde sans bruit
machine à capter ce silence
pour vous en mettre dans l'oreille
à grands coups d'ailes inutiles.

Qui possède quoi?

Qui possède quoi dans ces enclos? A qui est-ce
la montagne investie jusqu'au sommet,
les murs patients, les blés jaunes, les amandiers?
Serait-ce à toi, à toi, ce beau domaine,
la maison, la pièce d'eau précieuse,
l'enfant qui crie sur la pelouse?
Ah, qui saura retenir entre ses mains
les murs qui tombent, la fleur immuable,
les héritages démembrés, les puits taris?
Des familles éteintes qui lira les noms
sur la mousse des tombes oubliées?
Et le vent, les rochers, et la mort, à qui est-ce?

7 mai 1956

Useless Machine

A machine to make noise
that snorts and begs and proclaims
not only to keep you quiet
perhaps not to amuse me
built out of alien words
to discolor one by the other
to enter the depth of the grain
to pierce all the grains
to pass through the holes
to draw the impregnable water
whose course roars without noise
a machine to capture this silence
to put some of it in your ear
with a great fluttering of useless wings.

Who Owns What?

Who owns what in these enclosures? Who owns
that mountain fenced in to the top,
the patient walls, the golden wheat, the almond tree?
Would they be yours, yours this handsome property,
that house that pretty little pond,
the child crying on the lawn?
Ah! who will know how to hold in his hands
the falling walls, the immutable flower,
the dismembered inheritances, the wells gone dry?
Who will read the names of these dead families
on the moss of forgotten tombs?
And the wind, the rocks, and death, to whom do they
belong?

Espagne

Râpée et rose, toute mouchetée
d'yeuses maigres et le sang invisible
sous la craie blanche qui criait,
comme une jument pleine
de force vaine,
et pleine d'un squelette pétrifié. Rien,
Espagne, rien
que mille chiens errants,
parmi les ânes, partout, petits amis vaillants.
Je les bâterais avec dedans ma grande âme vaine,
tous nos malheurs, fardeaux si minuscules,
au bord du blason énorme sur la tour,
vaniteux de la gloire.

L'ânon rêve d'un mieux-être, pensif,
et le petit garçon,
cul-nu sur la croupe regarde,
entre ses doigts
à travers le vert violent. Rien.
Tu dors, figée parmi les blasons
gladiolés des parcours anciens.
Et les charrues passent par les sillons,
les araires d'un creusement révolu.

Les châteaux se dressent, squelettes d'aigles,
parmi le vert violent et la pierre. L'aire
où l'on bat le blé insuffisant
resplendit à Zamarramala, vaine.
Les bœufs noirs conduisent les chars de foin. Au soir
les troupeaux moutonnent sur les berges,
ils entrent dans l'eau, dans la ville. La vie.
Et rien, Espagne, rien. Honneur et mourir.

1955

Spain

Threadbare and pink, all speckled
with slender live-oaks and invisible blood
beneath the white chalk that shrieks
like a mare full
of useless energy,
full of a petrified skeleton. Nothing,
Spain, nothing
but a thousand wandering dogs,
among the donkeys, everywhere, brave little friends.
I will load them with inside my great empty soul,
all our pains, such tiny burdens,
at the edge of the huge coat-of-arms on the tower,
eager for glory.

The foal dreams of a better world, pensive,
and the little boy,
hunched bare-ass on the rump
looks through his fingers
toward the violent green. Nothing.
You sleep, set among the blazons
gladiolus along the old paths.
And the plows pass over the furrows,
the plowshare has finished its plowing.

The castles arise, skeletons of eagles,
in the midst of the violent green and the rock. The floor
where the scanty wheat is threshed
shines in Zamarramala, empty.
Black cattle draw the hay carts. At night
the flocks whiten the banks,
they cross the water, the town. Life.
And nothing, Spain, nothing. Honor and death.

Les morts sont toujours jeunes et la vie ardemment pâlit

Mon père depuis que tu es mort
c'est toi qui es devenu mon petit enfant

Je te vois entouré des draperies funéraires
conservant le patrimoine de fierté sur ton visage
les pâtures et les bois étendus près de ton lit
Et tu es incertain
parce que tu m'avais voulu éclairé selon ta loi
Et je suis devant toi tout brouillé par la détresse
Dans mes yeux troubles une énergie que tu ne peux peser

Le plus noble regard qu'un homme ait laissé à un autre
Et moi rongé par les bêtes mes rayons difficiles
sans œuvre inscrite que d'avoir tout perdu
Je n'ai pas de répondants que tu puisses accepter
et moi-même je ne suis pas sûr de mes témoins
Un risible un rêveur échoué qui ne te l'aura dit
avec ces paroles qui me sortent des statues de vent
oscillant entre la facilité et l'impossible
sans passer par les lieux où les hommes rompent leur pain

Après tant d'années où je n'ai pas pu
à cause des larmes
le jour est venu où plus fort dans les périls
j'ose m'avancer pour te rendre hommage
et devant toi me justifier comme j'en ai besoin

Alors je me tenais isolé dans ma fureur
sans bien distinguer entre la droiture sans entaille
et les vieilles armoiries démantelées
agité parmi les tremblements et les perspectives
contestable comme l'est un homme dans le désordre
à sa révolte plus d'insultes que de raisons

The dead are always young and life ardently pales

My father ever since your death
you have become my little child

I see you among the funeral drapes
keeping the heritage of pride on your face
the pastures and woods stretch out near your bed
And you are uncertain
because you wanted me wise according to your law
And here I stand in front of you confused by distress
In my troubled eyes an energy you cannot weigh

The noblest look that a man has left to another
And I gnawed by animals my troublesome shelves
without written work but having lost everything
I have no guarantors you can accept
and neither am I sure of my own witnesses
A joker, a stranded dreamer who would not have spoken
with these words that come to me from statues of wind
oscillating between facility and the impossible
without passing through those places where men break their bread

After so many years when I could not
because of tears
the day came when stronger in danger
I dare come closer to render you homage
and justify myself before you as I must

Once I kept to myself in my anger
unable to see the difference between rectitude without a fault
and the old dismantled armorial bearings
troubled by the tremblings and the perspectives
questionable like a man living in a state of disorder
about his revolt more of insults than reasons

Il y a si longtemps que j'ai refusé votre ordre
et la croix qui le somme du dieu étendu
cadavre de gloire au malheur duquel
il faut compatir pour qu'il nous console

Mais Dieu n'est pas mort Il n'est pas C'est moi qui meurs
Il naît lui Il n'en finira jamais de naître
non pas votre dieu mais un autre inconnu
parmi l'agonie de notre vie respirant
parmi les frémissements et les rocs jusqu'aux nuages
celui qui ne prend pas de figure

Celui-ci n'est pas facile à honorer Il le faut
Je dois prendre part à son accomplissement
Je suis fait responsable par le temps
Sur notre terre En danger Seul
Il ne viendra de renfort que d'entre nous
Il n'y aura pas d'ascension

Je n'ai pas de mission à remplir mais je suis là
acharné à m'ériger à partir de mes bas lieux
jusqu'à rompre ma consistance pour vivre en vraie vie
Je résiste de toutes les forces de mon opacité
Je dois me faire mon maître par la nuit mon bourreau
Les épines la couronne tous les instruments sont à moi
Justifié je peux l'être dans l'espace de ma journée
si de mon insuffisance je ne prends le parti

J'ai peiné dans la peine des autres et dans la mienne
Dans le désert non désirable de l'amour
je me suis battu
Insatisfait jusque du bonheur j'ai affreusement ri
Je me suis provoqué de cent manières
J'ai fléchi j'ai fait face je n'ai pas eu la force
Je suis vaincu Je n'abandonnerai jamais
Je poursuis éclatant parmi mes vomissures
Cette sorte de victoire que je veux gagner

I refused your order so long ago
and the cross which summons it from the knowledge of god
corpse of glory whose woes
we must bear to be consoled by him

But God is not dead He is not It is I who dies
He will rise He will always rise
not your god but another unknown
in the agony of our life breathing
among the rustlings and the rocks touching the clouds
he who remains faceless

This one is not easy to honor It must be done
I must take part in his fulfilment
Time has made me responsible
On our earth In danger Alone
No help will come but from ourselves
There will be no ascension

I have no mission to accomplish but I am here
desperately trying to constitute myself from the ground up
to the point of going mad to live my true life
I resist with all the powers of my opacity
I must become my own master at night my executioner
The thorns the crown all the instruments are mine
Justified I could be in the space of a day
if I were not to take sides with my weakness

I grieved in the grief of others and in my own
In the undesirable desert of love
I have struggled
Unsatisfied to the point of happiness I have laughed hideously
I challenged myself in a hundred ways
I weakened I faced it I did not have the strength
I am beaten I shall never surrender
Brilliant I pursue in my own vomit
This sort of victory that I want to earn

quand viendra la fin
j'aurai tenté du moins d'en marquer le prix

J'ai dépassé le milieu de ma vie j'ai persisté
Ce que tous vous appelez l'ordre notre échec
à haute voix mensongère légiférant
et qui tient Éternel encore s'il change
je ne l'accepte pas plus que mon édifice tremblant

Comment n'aurais-je pas cru au rêve de lutter ensemble
C'était pour nous établir en harmonie
Quand les grandes promesses retombées sur nous
en drapeaux méprisants
nous ont bafoués
fidèle à l'homme sans plus l'espoir
de déjouer l'irrémédiable
que reste-t-il hors de témoigner selon ses forces

Que porté-je dans les mains qui sache bruire
Quelle profonde musique
à laquelle seraient les hommes redevables
assez douloureuse et resplendissant pour les émouvoir
Mais qui saura m'assurer s'ils y retrouvent
notre tragique innocence notre vraie bonté
donateur dans l'incertitude

Je ne veux justifier ma vie que par ma vie
Je n'ai pas eu pitié de moi
J'ai subvenu autant qu'il faut à ma fureur
fragile inébranlable portant toute ma charge
au long de l'impossible dessein

J'ai repoussé la main des dieux:
je suis un homme digne de vivre
Si notre lumière est froide si je le sais
alors je peux me réjouir
Les oiseaux rient parfois les visages embellissent

when the end comes
I shall have tried at least to mark the prize

I have passed my middle years I have persisted
What all of you call order, our defeat
with a high lying voice legislating
and which holds Eternity though it changes.
I accept it no more than my own trembling edifice

How could I not have believed in the dream of fighting together
We were going to live in harmony
When the great promises fell back on us
like contemptuous flags
jeered us
faithful to man without any hope
of thwarting the irremediable
what remains but to stand each according to his strength

What did I carry in my hand that could hum
What profound music
to which men would be beholden
sufficiently sorrowful and resplendent to move them
But who will convince me if they discover there
our tragic innocence our true goodness
giver in uncertainty

I only want to justify my life by my life
I have had no pity on myself
I provided everything necessary for my fury
fragile steadfast carrying all my burdens
to the end of the impossible plan

I have repulsed the hand of the gods:
I am a man worthy to live
If our light is cold if I know it
then I can rejoice
Birds laugh sometimes faces brighten

Des yeux dans d'autres yeux mille arbres ont grandi
Je n'ai pas peur La dignité impie a bon visage
Je suis parmi les hommes dans l'inutile cargaison
Je ne méprise aucun de ceux qui sont ici
Il n'excèdera jamais mes forces
de respecter l'honneur des autres
Ma vie toujours menacée
par la haine de moi toujours fraîche
Les répits ne durent pas le bonheur
L'effort maintenu laisse incertain m'affaiblit
Et ceci qui ne m'importait pas maintenant m'importe
car j'approche

Le plus noble regard qu'un homme ait laissé à un autre

Toi qui n'avais fait tort à personne jamais
tu savais bien que j'essaierais de ne rien gâcher
si difficile que soit l'intégrité sans espérance

Père perdu
je recevais de toi dans le temps où je m'opposais
mais peut-être le malheur était nécessaire
que tu partes
afin de me donner davantage
si nous n'acquérons rien que dans le regret
ou par l'impossible désir

Je n'ai pas cessé de me tenir avec toi
A chaque pas je te reconnais qui me guides
sur un chemin que tu n'as pas suivi
mon père unique le seul compagnon paternel
O noblesse du cœur haut soleil exemplaire
aux distances les plus lointaines réapparaissant
si on l'a une fois connu
O père c'est ma vie qui te garde en vie pour que tu l'éclaires
Tu disparaîtras quand je ne serai plus

Eyes in other eyes a thousand trees have grown
I am not afraid Impious dignity wears well
I am among men in this worthless cargo
I do not despise anyone who is here
It will never exceed my strength
to respect the honor of others
My life always menaced
by a self-hate always replenished
The respites shorter than the happiness
The constant effort leaves uncertain weakens me
And what was then unimportant now seems important to me
because I am coming closer

The noblest look that a man has left to another

You who had never wronged anyone
you knew well enough that I would not try to spoil anything
even though integrity without hope is such a difficult thing

Father gone
even while I opposed you I received from you
but perhaps misfortune was necessary
you had to go
in order to give me more
if we acquire nothing but in regret
or by an impossible desire

I have never stopped standing by your side
Each step I take I recognize who guides me
on a path you have not followed
my true father my only paternal companion
O the heart's nobility exemplary high sun
in the furthest distances reappearing
if one has only known it once
O father it is my life that keeps you alive so that you may light it
You will disappear when I will be no more

Toujours liés nous deux Jusque là on ne se quitte pas

Va Je ne suis pas indigne d'aller te rejoindre
là-bas où un homme n'en rencontre un autre plus jamais.

Paris 1939, 1947 et 1951–1952

Les Fils bleus du temps

Les fils bleus du temps
t'ont mêlée à mes tempes
Toujours je me souviendrai
de ta chevelure

Après l'amertume
tant d'autres pas vides
loin par-delà l'oubli
mort de tant de morts
si même vivant
un éclat de ton œil clair
est monté dans mon regard
toute l'ardeur de ta beauté
se répand même à voix basse
dans tous les jours de ma voix
un signe épars dans mon miroir transformé
une douceur dans la confusion de mes songes
une chaleur par les seins froids de ma nuit

Je meurs de ma vie
je n'ai pas fini
Je te porterai encore
mon feu amour.

Always together we two Until that time we shall not part

Go I am not unworthy of following you
There where a man never meets another man.

The Blue Threads of Time

The blue threads of time
have tangled you in my temples
Always I shall remember
your hair

After bitterness
so many other empty steps
on the far side of forgetfulness
death of so many deaths
even if alive
a flash from your clear eye
arose in my sight
all the ardor of your beauty
can be heard even in low voices
in all the days of my voice
a lost sign transformed in my mirror
a softness in the confusion of my dreams
a warmth by the cold breasts of my night

I die of my life
I have not finished
I bring you still
my late love.

L'Irruption des mots

Je ris aux mots J'aime quand ça démarre
qu'ils s'agglutinent et je les déglutis
comme cent cris de grenouillles en frai
Ils sautent et s'appellent
s'éparpillent et m'appellent
et se rassemblent et je ne sais
si c'est Je qui leur réponds ou eux encore
dans un tumulte intraitablement frais
qui vient sans doute de mes profondes lèvres
là-bas où l'eau du monde m'a donné vie
Je me vidange quand m'accouchent ces dieux têtards.
Je m'allège et m'accrois par ces sons qui dépassent
issus d'un au-delà presque tout préparés
J'en fais le tour après enorgueilli
ne me reconnaissant qu'à peine en ce visage
qu'ils m'ont fait voir et qui parfois m'effraie
car ce n'est pas moi seul qui par eux me démange.

27 janvier 1948

The Irruption of Words

I laugh at words I like it when the action starts
when they agglutinate and I ingurgitate
like the hundred cries of spawning frogs
They leap and call out
scatter and call me
and come together and I don't know
if it is I who answer them or they themselves
in a tumult uncompromisingly fresh
that must undoubtedly come from my deepest lips
there where the water of the world gave me life
I drain myself when these godly tadpoles deliver me.
I feel lighter and grow by these distant sounds
arising almost perfect from a beyond
Afterward I proudly strut among them
hardly recognizing myself in that face
they have made me see and which sometimes frightens me
for they are not the only reason why I itch.

Yves Bonnefoy

Born 1923 in Tours

There is a degree of tolerance in the act of speaking: errors, confusion, retrospective analyses, tangential excursions, insights into obscure regions, unforeseen conjunctions, a fortiori *reasoning—all of this may occur and exist for a moment. But when Yves Bonnefoy speaks, the listener is first attentive to the harmonious quality of his voice, the eloquence that shuns the coarser word and that selects the elegant substitute, the particular vocabulary that will suit his expression. And there is a rythmic pattern, a broken and continuous thrust that establishes a tonal line, affirming by its physical presence the concreteness of the often highly abstract nature of the subject matter. The gravity of the voice, the poise, the evolution, the complexity of his thought add to the cumulative definition of the object as it momentarily assumes a form in the process of creation.*

The act of speaking is a dangerous one, a commitment with little chance of reversal, a cruel testimony to the manner in which the transient affects a degree of permanency. It is at once an occasion for the liberation of a thought and the invocation of haphazard words before they gain materiality. It would have been surprising for a poet whose work has appeared with such calculation to fall easy victim to an ex cathedra *pronouncement made into a recording machine. So Yves Bonnefoy, sitting in my office and smoking his cigarette, is in evident discomfort. As he speaks, he is listening to himself, and he corrects himself, and he is finally forced into silence, asking me to destroy part of the tape that did not conform to a perfectly shaped argument.*

Bonnefoy, like his poems, conceals an intense discipline. The words written and the words spoken have to be attuned to the same rigorous demands: there is a will to construct an exquisite medium that will impose itself and that will provide one of the keys to the proper approach to the verbal murals that are being outlined. Afraid that the speaking voice would not be true to the emplacement of his thought, Yves Bonnefoy decides to write out the interview, using the same questions, but now describing in a "natural" language his premeditated reflections. This extreme prudence is not only dictated by his philosophic training and his experience as a translator of Shakespeare, but also and essentially by the quality of the poetic com-

munication. Poetry is too adventurous a field to venture into without having first made sure of the required elements that will be both tool and object of discovery.

Would you be kind enough to situate yourself in French poetry from the time of the publication of your first work? Would you also discuss the differences and the resemblances between your own work and that of other contemporary poets?

I will try to answer your question, but I will have to simplify a good deal. I will also have to overcome a certain distaste I feel when I consider myself as an object to be analyzed and defined. What seems to me to characterize the poetic experience is precisely this refusal to approach a world where realities are reduced to their concepts. It is with this in mind that I try to create, though I would not want it to be thought that this was a conscious project when I began writing. Rather, I would say that it was the lesson contained in my earliest poems, obscurely animated by a will that I was only able to recognize little by little. But I convinced myself all the more from that time on that the intention of poetry, which differs in this from all other preoccupations of the consciousness, except for the religious one, is to tear away beings or things from the definitions or descriptions that fragment them, in order to give them back their proper identity. Or, as Blake said, their unity, their own presence. I would also add that this operation must first of all weigh on the person who is speaking. Presence in a world of presence all rustling with unity, or an object in an aggregate of objects silent and desolate—such is our double manner of being limited, and such is the alternative that poetry perceives in observing the condition of modern man.

Poetry is also the poem, which so often closes back unto itself, which reintroduces, on the level of creation, the sin of separation, of fragmentation, that poetry denounces in everyday existence. There is a conflict between this search for a presence and the interests of the work which can only accomplish its form by forgetting, as Mallarmé said, the existences that the poet encounters during his daily life and that he even tries to evoke, very sincerely, in what he is writing. Here I see an internal contradiction in all poetic enterprises, at least in our societies deprived of common rites; it is necessary to take a stand, and that is more or less what I tried to do with my poems *Anti-Platon*, the first that I published. There, I denounced nostalgia for the intelligible, which only transcribes our fear of what truly exists, here, now, within the scope of our existence. Why this fear? Because, in order to affront what exists, we must confront the evidence of death, we must throw ourselves in time . . .

What did you mean in one of your own texts when you spoke of the "thickness of the world?" Among many contemporary French poets there is a great desire to specify the value of an object. That is, the poets themselves have provided the "thickness" in order to regulate the relationships with the reality that surrounds them. In your own work, on the contrary, you appear to define the abyss, the void, the immaterial.

The thickness of the world? I know that a number of writers today hope to describe with precision and finesse the shape of things, or the links that these things thread between themselves and us. Because of this fact, these writers exist in a world of infinite appearances, and consequently they can discover, or create, the inexhaustible wealth of the aspect of whatever is there. But don't you agree that this proliferation is in fact a void, and we, in the center of it, an absence, where language alone remains truly in the act of *becoming*? This false "thickness" must cede before another evidence, which is the way, always near and always lost. The true "thickness" for me, is when one no longer sees the feathers of the bird, because, quite simply, the bird is here, with us; and if the different aspects of its body or of its flight, of its song, can be considered as the visible, well then, the present reality must be the invisible: it is an abyss opened onto the continuity of appearance, but it is also an abyss of concealed appearances. You no longer photograph; something has caught your attention. The visible is not erased: it has been liberated from itself. And though God knows it is not necessary to write poems in order to experience this, poetry retains this unformulated, or rather, fully formulated expression, and knows how to remember it, since it is the invisible bird and not the bird of the ornithologists which is evoked by the poetic word: *ici presque toujours si le ramier roucoule*, as Mallarmé wrote. It is because it is a presence that it haunts this place, and certainly not as one of the elements that allow it to be described. Had there been no wood-pigeon, something else in this place would have assumed the function of mourning. Poetry does not interest itself in the shape of the world in itself, but in the world that this universe will become. Poetry speaks only of presences—or absences.

In your critique of Baudelaire and Mallarmé, you say that the central problem in their works was one of temporality . . .

I believe that there is no approach nor any possible possession of the real except in time, through time. Finitude, that is to say, the limited character of our powers, of our existence in time, makes time the essential factor of our experience, as it does of life first of all, but also of things, which are perhaps more specifically associated with our experience than at first glance one would assume judging their classification, objective in character, intemporal.

Let me explain. Undoubtedly words, or things, only exist in relationship to each other, a process of differentiation opposes one to the other, and at the same time reunites them in a structure which appears to be non-temporal. But man, when he has differentiated the sky from the earth, has only managed to do this through the presence of the unity of the world which he penetrated with language, and with his life, which, at the same time, was separated from it and came back to it. And he has chosen these objects under the sign of this mystery. Words are the columns of a temple as they are of things. As far as science is concerned, neither wine nor bread can be exhausted, isn't that right? The conversion of time into eternity is written in filigree in the configuration that allows us to see the mountain or the river, rather than another object that a non-temporal observation (scientific, for example) might have found under natural conditions. And though we tend to forget it, time is the apparently "objective" secret of the universe. This permits me to underline, in passing, that a dramatic form of poetry that would deal with time, similar to the one that had appeared in Christianity, for example—a poetry that seems obsessed by the destiny of the individual—is *a priori* in no way separated from the perceptible wealth of the world, since only a preoccupation with destiny allows one to discover this profound economy which has constructed the real, the economy of bread and wine. No, this Baudelairian awareness of the clock, or of the "*jardins de cet astre*" that Mallarmé wants to praise, these are not exclusive one from the other, and what makes us understand one through the other, is our acceptance of death, which gives us back to ourselves, and to this universe, through love. Our language conceals, dissimulated today under the words of pure science, a voice. And the souvenir it keeps of it, and which asks us to act, but which is not really sufficient to transform us, is evidently poetry.

In referring to words and to this analogy with death, would you describe the origin of one of your own poems?

Yes. First, I might say that I do not write poems—if you mean by that something which has an autonomous existence, something self-sufficient. From the day that I became aware that words had become mine, that they no longer depended too heavily on the vision of other poets, but began to identify my own, to organize themselves through me—in fact, since that *Anti-Platon*, about which I spoke a while ago, and which formed itself brusquely, in an instant, like a chemical body that coagulates—well, from that day forward I no longer wrote poems but books, and this should not be construed as one long poem. These books do not grow out of a unity of form. At the beginning, I take note of a number of fragments of speech that impose themselves on me in a discontinuous and enigmatic manner. They come from me, but like a dream, they are still beyond the control of consciousness. Still, from one to the other of these presences, as soon as they are accepted, relationships are formed, a verbal space is sketched out, where their meanings that remain obscure, slowly become precise, despite themselves, and come to condense themselves into certain words or images.

I observe this structuration, but I have also begun to intervene, since it has become necessary to contribute to these simplifications, to aid in this need for coherence. The interpretation has already begun, and this may lead to a questioning of the first words by others that are more thought out, more explicit, generalized, that remember events, perceive analogies—but it is still true that it is from a number of transmitters and always in part undeciphered, that these networks of words take shape, and here I strongly feel that there are contradictions that I cannot accept, as long as a total form, in which all my existence has its place, and which depends on it, yes, which depends on my everyday acts, and which also depends on society, will not have come to resolve them. What is actual at this moment of writing is but the will toward unity! The intensity of the words and the immanence of the rhythm signify, before anything, this desire to mobilize oneself in order to achieve this projected unity. I have been able to express these tendencies that by themselves could not do it alone. But to express these tendencies, or constitute them in a verbal structure with many accesses, is not to compose them with all the others in a harmony which implicates me. I feel that it would be wrong to constrain these tensions, where, undoubtedly the great contradictions that tear modern man are marked, in order to freeze oneself in the unity of a poem that would really be just formal, and *happy*. What would be the sense of this unity? That I had been capable of choosing an "I" that would be able to compose these powers esthetically, according to the inspiration of a daydream, and consequently reduced to their appearances, and misunderstood in their depth which nevertheless had begun to speak. An "I" homogenous and unified would emerge, but unreal, outside of the time in which I remain, and deprived of an appreciation of the experiences of others, which was also in my words.

And as I mentioned, virtualities would lose themselves that depend on the living word, shared. The way of the sacred would be replaced by the way of beauty. . . . I believe it is better to allow these distinct voices to compete with each other on the open field. One can see that they illuminate each other, lending each other words. But the field of the non-formulated upon which they appear remains the essential, what is beyond the book within the book, the white sign that denounces the deceitful enclosures.

Of course, I realize that the construction of a work is as fatal as it is insidious. It may be that this opening, this discontinuity to which I believe I am faithful, is but an element along with others in a construction whose form now and always remains esthetic. In any case, I have observed that at the last moment, when many of the poems in a book had found their place and their meaning, a way appeared, an unexpected thought became a possible one: it was there, consequently in its power, although this new experience jeopardized the economy of the work itself. Thus, the book is a map—insufficient, and which cannot be anything else and which must remember that it is thus, partaking of the space of an existence, with, as a reason for being, our need for a true order, of a transparency in this ultimate and collective form of being, today and perhaps always inaccessible, that we call the sacred. Although it is still in its outlined form, it contributes to this harmony. But if we were to forget for a moment that it was but a map, an abstract, a meditation on traces, and this in order to bring together elements present in an ideal form, sufficient, and this "I" in its totality, universal which is discovering itself, which consults its sketches, its compass, then it would be, once again stifled, at the cost of a victory in the name of rhetoric.

Yet I do not exclude the possibility that the way to unity may occur brusquely—though for an instant only—on the occasion of simple acts. And thus the writer is capable of going beyond the discord of voices in himself with a few unifying words, a few basic symbols finally understood that seem to arrest, bring together the long history of his voice, and end the book in a condition of truth.

But why should the book still exist on the horizon of this music, when henceforth the simplest words suffice? Because one understands that the equilibrium thus found cannot last in a world like ours. We only come into contact with this state of presence at the crest of a duration which reaffirms itself and carries us away. The truth of these liberated moments remains within time and we must once again consult our pile of maps.

When do I consider a book finished? Perhaps when a number of alienations have presented themselves, or needs more precisely actual. Perhaps also when a number of partial resolutions of these conflicts have occurred, so that a stage has been reached on the road of life. I stopped writing *Douve*—and I mean by that *Douve* as a whole, certainly not the last poem—when this first exercise allowed me to gain confidence in the word. In the field of these forces, revealed by language, an event has occurred whose traces have blackened the stones here or there, and one wants to remember it. Of course one can also be wrong. The event might only have been a weariness or worse, the fear of an imminent revelation.

But it is also true that one is never finished with it. The book has hardly been published, that is to say, completed, when this stage is cleared by time which has not stopped. The voice of despair finds other proofs, for example, where a passion for form once again throws us off. And it is, besides, in this sliding, that the book reveals its true nature, which is to be an element among others in a vaster book whose horizon is the sense that one can give to one's life.

I do not write anything for two or three years after each book, because it seems to me that it is necessary to reinvent a language, considering that one is already another man. We must forget old words—which does not mean that we have to abandon them if they express our deepest nature—to reinvent them, to rediscover them in their thickness, at the cost of this mannerism which our fear of Being makes us accept. . . . Besides, only one word needs to be discovered in order for a whole language to change. Imperceptible births which serve us as proof of existence, our liberations of energy, our coming to the world, our duration more intensely lived. And one would not write were it not for this birth of words that gives us again the hope of a true life.

PRINCIPAL WORKS: *Traité du pianiste*, La Révolution la nuit, 1946
Du Mouvement et de l'immobilité de Douve, Mercure de France, 1953
Peintures murales de la France gothique, P. Hartmann, 1954
Hier régnant désert, Mercure de France, 1958
Pierre écrite, Maeght, 1959
L'Improbable, Essais, Mercure de France, 1959
La Seconde Simplicité, Mercure de France, 1961
Rimbaud par lui-même, coll. Ecrivains de Toujours. Ed. du Seuil, 1961
Pierre écrite, Mercure de France, 1964
Un rêve fait à Mantoue, Mercure de France, 1967

I

Je te voyais courir sur des terrasses,
Je te voyais lutter contre le vent,
Le froid saignait sur tes lèvres.

Et je t'ai vue te rompre et jouir d'être morte ô plus belle
Que la foudre, quand elle tache les vitres blanches de ton sang.

II

L'été vieillissant te gerçait d'un plaisir monotone, nous méprisions l'ivresse imparfaite de vivre.

«Plutôt le lierre, disais-tu, l'attachement du lierre aux pierres de sa nuit: présence sans issue, visage sans racine.

«Dernière vitre heureuse que l'ongle solaire déchire, plutôt dans la montagne ce village où mourir.

«Plutôt ce vent...»

III

Il s'agissait d'un vent plus fort que nos mémoires,
Stupeur des robes et cri des rocs—et tu passais devant ces flammes
La tête quadrillée les mains fendues et toute
En quête de la mort sur les tambours exultants de tes gestes.

C'était jour de tes seins
Et tu régnais enfin absente de ma tête.

I

I saw you running on the terraces,
I saw you struggle against the wind,
The cold bloodied your lips.

And I saw you break apart and rejoice in your death o more beautiful
Than thunder, when it marks the white panes with your blood.

II

Aging summer parched you with a monotonous pleasure, we despised the imperfect ecstasy of living.

"Rather the ivy, you said, the fondness of the ivy for the rocks of its night: presence without issue, face without roots.

"Last blessed window torn by the solar claw, rather in the mountain this village where we die.

"Rather this wind . . ."

III

We were dealing with a wind far stronger than our memories,
Stupor of clothing and the cry of rocks—and you walked in front of
  the flames
Your head checkered your hands broken and all
In search of death on the exultant drums of your gestures.

It was the day of your breasts
And you reigned at last absent from my mind.

IV

Je me réveille, il pleut. Le vent te pénètre, Douve, lande résineuse endormie près de moi. Je suis sur une terrasse, dans un trou de la mort. De grands chiens de feuillages tremblent.

Le bras que tu soulèves, soudain, sur une porte, m'illumine à travers les âges. Village de braise, à chaque instant je te vois naître, Douve,

A chaque instant mourir.

V

Le bras que l'on soulève et le bras que l'on tourne
Ne sont d'un même instant que pour nos lourdes têtes,
Mais rejetés ces draps de verdure et de boue
Il ne reste qu'un feu du royaume de mort.

La jambe démeublée où le grand vent pénètre
Poussant devant lui des têtes de pluie
Ne vous éclairera qu'au seuil de ce royaume,
Gestes de Douve, gestes déjà plus lents, gestes noirs.

VI

Quelle pâleur te frappe, rivière souterraine, quelle artère en toi se rompt, où l'écho retentit de ta chute?

Ce bras que tu soulèves soudain s'ouvre, s'enflamme. Ton visage recule. Quelle brume croissante m'arrache ton regard? Lente falaise d'ombre, frontière de la mort.

Des bras muets t'accueillent, arbres d'une autre rive.

IV

I awake, it is raining. The wind goes through you, Douve, resinous field asleep at my side. I am on a terrace, in a trough of death. Great dogs of leaves are trembling.

The arm you raise, suddenly, against a door, lights me across the ages. Village of embers, at every moment I see your birth, Douve,

At every moment your death.

V

The arms raised and the arm turned
Share the same instant only for our heavy heads,
But thrown aside these sheets of greenery and mud
Only a fire remains from the kindgom of death.

The empty leg where the great wind enters
Pushing in front of it heads of rain
Will only light your way at the threshold of this kingdom,
Douve's gestures, gestures already slower, black gestures.

VI

What pallor strikes you, subterranean river, what artery breaks within you, where the echo rings with your fall?

The arm that you raise suddenly opens, catches fire. Your face recedes. What thickening fog tears your face away from me? Slow cliff of shadow, frontier of death.

Silent arms greet you, trees of another shore.

VII

Blessée confuse dans les feuilles,
Mais prise par le sang de pistes qui se perdent,
Complice encor du vivre.

Je t'ai vue ensablée au terme de ta lutte
Hésiter aux confins du silence et de l'eau,
Et la bouche souillée des dernières étoiles
Rompre d'un cri l'horreur de veiller dans ta nuit.

O dressant dans l'air dur soudain comme une roche
Un beau geste de houille.

Une Voix

Écoute-moi revivre dans ces forêts
Sous les frondaisons de mémoire
Où je passe verte,
Sourire calciné d'anciennes plantes sur la terre,
Race charbonneuse du jour.

Écoute-moi revivre, je te conduis
Au jardin de présence,
L'abandonné au soir et que des ombres couvrent,
L'habitable pour toi dans le nouvel amour.

Hier régnant désert, j'étais feuille sauvage
Et libre de mourir,
Mais le temps mûrissait, plainte noire des combes,
La blessure de l'eau dans les pierres du jour.

Oh, quel feu dans le pain rompu, quelle aube
Pure dans les étoiles affaiblies !
Je regarde le jour venir parmi les pierres,
Tu es seule dans ta blancheur vêtue de noir.

VII

Wounded lost among the leaves,
But caught up by the blood of trails that disappear,
Accomplice yet of living.

I saw you covered with sand at the end of your struggle
Hesitating at the edge of silence and water,
And your mouth soiled by the last stars
Break with a cry the horror of watching through your night.

O rising in the hard air sudden as a rock
A gesture of coal.

A Voice

Hear me live again in these forests
Under the foliage of memory
Where I pass green,
Charred smile of old plants on earth,
Charcoal race of day.

Hear me live again, I bring you
To the garden of presence,
The abandoned at night and covered with shadows
The place for you in your new love.

Yesterday the desert reigned, I was a wild leaf
And free to die,
But time ripened, black cry of the valleys,
The wound of water in the stones of the day.

Oh, what fire in the broken bread, what a pure
Dawn among the paling stars!
I watch the day coming among the rocks,
You are alone in your whiteness dressed in black.

Aube, fille des larmes, rétablis
La chambre dans sa paix de chose grise
Et le cœur dans son ordre. Tant de nuit
Demandait à ce feu qu'il décline et s'achève,
Il nous faut bien veiller près du visage mort.
A peine a-t-il changé... Le navire des lampes
Entrera-t-il au port qu'il avait demandé,
Sur les tables d'ici la flamme faite cendre
Grandira-t-elle ailleurs dans une autre clarté?
Aube, soulève, prends le visage sans ombre,
Colore peu à peu le temps recommencé.

La même voix, toujours

Je suis comme le pain que tu rompras,
Comme le feu que tu feras, comme l'eau pure
Qui t'accompagnera sur la terre des morts.

Comme l'écume
Qui a mûri pour toi la lumière et le port.

Comme l'oiseau du soir qui efface les rives,
Comme le vent du soir soudain plus brusque et froid.

L'Oiseau des ruines

L'oiseau des ruines se sépare de la mort,
Il nidifie dans la pierre grise au soleil,
Il a franchi toute douleur, toute mémoire,
Il ne sait plus ce qu'est demain dans l'éternel.

Dawn, daughter of tears, restore
The room to its calm of gray things
And the heart to its place. So much night
Called the fire to weaken and go out,
We really should keep watch near the dead face.
It has hardly changed . . . Will the ship of lamps
Enter the harbor it had asked for,
On these tables the flame turns to ashes
Will it grow elsewhere in another light?
Dawn, lift up, take the face without shadow,
Little by little color time renewed.

The Same Voice, Always

I am like the bread you shall break,
Like the fire you shall make, like the pure water
That will go with you in the land of the dead.

Like the foam
That has ripened for you the light and the harbor.

Like the evening bird that erases the shores,
Like the evening wind suddenly sharper and cold.

The Bird in the Ruins

The bird in the ruins breaks away from death,
It nestles in the gray rock in the sun,
It is beyond all suffering, all memory,
It no longer knows what is tomorrow in eternity.

André du Bouchet

Born 1924 in Paris

In the absence of certainty, André du Bouchet proceeds with caution. His few poems are fixed on the page, in defiance and in deference, and there they exist, impressing their contours on the whiteness, forcing the eye and the mind to establish a relevance between the statement and the hazardous progress represented by the book of poems.

André du Bouchet—ascetic, mild-mannered, incisive, self-critical—questions each of his assertions as he proves them, works over and over until he has created an unimpeachable presence, something, a voice in this instance, which speaks with the hesitating lurches and the backward stepping of an authentic perturbation.

It is clear from his crouched position and from his own interpellation that he does not like being questioned—that he rebels against this evidence that he is forced to give, out of a sense of courtesy, and he gives it, he changes directions, like those lines in his poems that all of a sudden shift, cut back, go breakingly forward, and then stop. Like a fascinated spectator, I try to anticipate the next twist, the next evasion that is a valid statement of the profoundly unsteadying quality of du Bouchet's poetry. The hesitancy comes from his suspicion of global affirmations. What becomes classified is no longer essentially meaningful. He makes the same observations about the nature of the words that he uses. (Bonnefoy would have agreed.) The absence of finality in his own views corresponds to his refusal to fraternize too freely with literature as a closed object.

Now we pause in this austere room that resembles his poems. Absence of topicality. A forceful presence, a clarity that comes into view. The light is even. A few paintings accentuate the fragility of the moment.

When the tape runs out, the tension disappears. I find myself confronted by a person whose extreme self-exposure has caused me both great joy and great exhaustion. As demanding as his work, du Bouchet has proceeded to the limit of the tape, establishing by his very disconcerting replies, an irreplaceable tone to his voice, and a mood that could not be duplicated. All the obstacles that have surged into his poems have appeared in his unrehearsed voice: earthbound, tracking; this man respects solar energy.

Where would you place yourself in the current of French poetry since the end of the war?

I have the feeling that I cannot in any way place myself, and in trying to write, in this work that sometimes ends with a poem, or does not, each time this effort represents an attempt to place myself, but the result is never achieved. So that I do not place myself except within the poem that I am trying to write and which often does not lead anywhere. Besides, it is with difficulty that I see what you mean when you speak about French poetry. I do not see this activity that is called poetry as something very distinct from the activity of other men who are known as novelists or painters. Often as I read (and when you speak about reading it implies poetry or the history of poetry), I find (as I have after discovering the works of Tolstoy, all of whose works I have read in translation) that I had discovered (even though this body of work is materially immense and one would never dream of placing it in the category of poetry)—that it had the feeling of something very elusive and yet very precise at the same time, and which seemed to me not to differ from what happened in poetry. And I deliberately mention Tolstoy because he is not a French poet writing between 1945 and 1965. So . . . I do not find myself in line with any particular school. This idea of "French poetry" is rather strange to me. I have more tenacious centers of interests, more persistent ones; I do not reread a poem, a poet twice in the same manner. But, through a diversity of approaches, there is a sort of polarization or constant centers that are revealed. But I would find it very difficult to identify these permanent elements, these constant elements, since after all, they probably reflect me. That is exactly what I am trying to render with greater precision, trying to localize.

And if I have got to refer to my own past, I remember that when I was a child I read a lot of poetry and then, around sixteen or seventeen, I chanced upon an anthology of poets who were almost my contemporaries, that is, the Surrealists. It was in 1943 or '44, and that anthology seemed to me to be absolutely incomprehensible. I remember very well having had the following thought: "If that is poetry, then I am not a poet." And I had exactly the opposite feeling a little while later, when again, completely by chance, I read Reverdy.

Then I had the feeling of a perfect clarity which existed for me; I could gain access to the poems on a sure footing, and they were at the same time parallel to my own personal experiences and simultaneously made the link with what I liked in the works of much older poets, like Baudelaire, and others, older still. And all of a sudden there was no more need of a solution to continuity. As you can see, I turn in circles. I do not place myself in any way in a movement or in a time, or in any sort of temporal succession.

About Tolstoy and Reverdy . . .

Isn't it sufficient to speak of Tolstoy and Reverdy in the same breath? This joining of the two is perfectly preposterous. These two names reveal that there can be no question of literary history, or order or sequences in literature or in poetry as it is considered in books. It is a question of something that is completely imponderable and which is for me the order of existence that I feel at the same time in Reverdy and in Tolstoy but which appears absolutely absurd the minute these two names are brought together, since they apparently have nothing in common. I would not even take a chance and try to define what, if anything, they may have in common. Nevertheless, I feel in the constancy of my interest in both something which does not have a name . . .

Is it possible that what you find in the one and the other, as well as in other poets that you have not mentioned, would be in part their perfection, that is, that extreme richness which is found in Tolstoy's style, and perhaps, if you are touched by it, his moral judgements, his ethics . . . a richness that has to do with his vision . . .

Perhaps if these two names come to mind, it is that in the two works there is nothing in common: that may be their common point, that may be the reason for their extraordinary persistence. Both of their works have an extraordinary center, a basis around which the author has localized himself, and it is in this depth, this center which remains elusive each time one reads their works, and that one has a great difficulty in defining as had Tolstoy and Reverdy when they experienced it; it is then this center of resistance which perhaps holds me more than the work itself. If I were to say that I was particularly attracted by the work itself, then the coming together of the works of Tolstoy and Reverdy would appear in all of its flagrant absurdity. I suppose that is all I have got to say . . .

In your own work, when you try to discover in yourself that center which you appreciate in others, are you capable of defining it? Can you isolate it?

The poem defines it. I would say that in the course of years, one comes to this conclusion: The need to familiarize oneself with the ways of gaining access to oneself. In the end, one gets to know oneself a little bit. But if this work, where one is seeking oneself, and in the course of which one recognizes oneself, must end, then the result to which it leads is a sort of immediate contradiction to this familiarity, and it then happens that one discovers something new that one did not know before, otherwise it would only be repetitive. It would be purely and simply a repetition and finally a sort of dupery. Why continue? Why repeat what has already been said, you might say that what characterizes this fact of existence is that there are no "constant values." As long as one is alive, there are always new things, as long as one is alive . . .

A number of younger poets are particularly interested in language per se, a pursuit rather distant from social motives: where would you situate yourself in this area?

For my part, language is not at all the object of my work. I do not work at all on the level of language, or a structure of language; I try to translate other things but then again it is certainly not Man that interests me when I speak of Tolstoy or Reverdy as such—that is, to take two names at random where one could cite others, I am not searching for the man in the work but the man in the manner in which he is centered in his work, in his poetry, taken in the largest sense of the word, or his poetry when it succeeds in localizing this man, so furtive, and also so elusive, so that there is something that is not exactly . . . which goes beyond the domain which is, strictly speaking, that of man. I am not interested in the man Tolstoy or the man Reverdy in the way they were then known and in the way they appeared in the accounts of the period, in the souvenirs or the journals of people who knew them. It is not that man in particular that I try to find in reading his works, but the center in that work which remains elusive, consequently alive for the reader, as elusive and alive as it was for the author at the moment when he was trying to find himself by means of the work. To the degree that in writing, man goes beyond what he is, one operates on the level of language, but one does not stop with language: language is not an end in itself. It remains open, consequently, it remains open on something that is other than language. If there is examination of language, it is not as a closed structure.

Isn't the very title "Chaleur vacante" an expression of a more profound origin, implying a sort of metaphysical area? That vacancy, that absence of repetition which you have tried to define, is it not perhaps what we are now trying to define?

Yes, yes . . . since you're quoting it. It is, basically, what we've been saying. It is the idea of a closed world which supposes heat and which burns and which is at the same time available and which does not feed upon itself but which also supposes this opening onto the world and which participates in this combustion which is more generalized and which is not, strictly speaking, personal.

The image of fire, of course, goes back at least to the Greeks, and then evolves through the Middle Ages. It has all sorts of connotative meanings. Do you see yourself pursuing any one of those significances when you allude so frequently to fire?

Yes. I see the word—every time I see the word fire and heat, and god knows they are often used. I recognize them when others use them, but this does not mean that they belong to a system or that I use them because I have read them.

But don't you feel when you write about fire, or about walls, so often present in your poems, that you're trying to affirm something? Isn't there some force . . .?

Yes, after having written it, after having written it to the degree that it has been written, it becomes dead weight and it falls in that domain that I mentioned a while ago, when I was saying that I try to avoid the familiarity of a word. It augurs ill when a word is recognized, acquired, returns too frequently . . .

Once the poem has been constituted, do you see a relationship, a sort of integral relationship with other poems?

There it is a question of creating a sort of link that one feels but that one could not know in advance existed with other things that have been written, and this link, completely unexpected, which must occur between the poem that one has just written and others that one has written, answers, basically, to that unknown continuity which is that of our own existence. It is impossible to foresee a collection of poems, as impossible as it is to foresee one's own existence . . .

PRINCIPAL WORKS: *Au deuxième étage*, Le Dragon, 1946
Le Moteur blanc, G.L.M. 1946, 1948
Sans couvercle, G.L.M. 1953
Cette Surface, Alès: Impr. Benoit, 1956
Sol de la montagne, Jean Hughes, 1956
Dans la chaleur vacante, Mercure de France, 1959, 1961
Sur le pas, Iliazd, 1960
Poèmes de Hölderlin, traduction, Mercure de France, 1963
Ou le Soleil, Mercure de France, 1968

L'Air soudain

Au pied de ce mur que l'ombre défait, l'ombre
attend,
de ce ciel.

Cette blancheur furieuse, la nuit,
le souffle
qui me sépare de mon lit.

L'horizon diffus,
à la coupure du souffle. J'avance dans le
jour retentissant.

La maison s'anime. L'air se fend.

Relief

Aujourd'hui la lampe parle

elle a pris une couleur
violente
tout éclate et rayonne
et sert
jusqu'aux miettes

la soucoupe blanche
que je vois sur la table
que l'air modèle

la vérité morte
froide
vivante maintenant

Suddenly Air

At the foot of this wall that a shadow destroys, the shadow waits,
out of this sky.

This furious whiteness, the night,
the breath
that separates me from my bed.

The diffuse horizon,
at the cut of the breath. I go into the ringing day.

The house comes alive. The air breaks.

Relief

Today the lamp speaks

it has taken on a violent
color
everything bursts and shines
and serves
even the crumbs

the white saucer
that I see on the table
that the air shapes

the dead truth
cold
and yet alive

et sans arrêt

à voix haute.

La neige de notre respiration
fond

vivant

au ralenti

comme une table

dans la lumière sauvage de l'écorce

nature vivante
déjà hier
sur un rayon

avec des vêtements secs.

Sûr de refleurir

rien ne dérangera
l'ombre
de ma chambre

avec des seaux de froid
en haut
d'une montagne d'air
qui ressemble à un seau

elle tremble
comme une lampe

j'éclaire

and without stopping

out loud.

The snow of our breathing
melts

alive

slowed down

like a table

in the savage light of the bark

vivid landscape
already yesterday
on a shelf

with dry clothing.

Sure of flowering again

nothing will upset
the shadow
of my room

with pails of cold
on top
of a mountain of air
that resembles a pail

it trembles
like a lamp

I light

je vois

des lettres

sur cette table
sauvage.

Sol de la montagne

Le courant force

se risquer dans le jour
comme dans l'eau
froide et blanche

dure
pour le motocycliste

comme un couteau déplacé par le souffle

les montagnes sortent à peine de terre

quand la route casse
je change de pied

elle est couverte de neige.

I see

letters

on this savage
table.

Mountain Terrain

The current pushes

to take a chance with the day
as with the water
cold and white

hard
for the motorcyclist

like a knife displaced by the wind

the mountains barely emerge from the earth

when the road stumbles
I change my footing

it is covered with snow.

Rudiments

1

Force
ou génie de la toux

incroyable glacier.

2

Rester au niveau, à quelques pouces du front, dans le feu infirme.

Comme un arbre dans le froid, le mur franchi se perd aussi, vraie peinture.

Les mains que ce même vent, le soir,
arrêté sur la route,
brûle.

3

Ce balbutiement blanc

cette bulle

la figure
encore criblée de pierres

à côté de chaque roue

dans la paille

qui craque

près de la lumière.

Rudiments

1

Force
or genius of the cough

unbelievable glacier.

2

To stay at the level, a few inches from the front, in the weak fire.

Like a tree in the cold, the wall also passes loses itself, true painting.

These hands that the same wind, at night,
stopped on the road,
burns.

3

This white mumbling

this bubble

the face
still riddled with stones

next to each wheel

in the hay

cracking

near the light.

4

Le feu

ce feu
qui reprend
derrière la terre fermée

je referme la porte blanche

le souffle
qui sort du champ

la lumière

la bride.

5

Au pire,
l'orage endormi contre un mur. La montagne, le caillou qui ensevelit la montagne.

Quand la nuit tombe, la route inutile est couverte de pays noirs qui se multiplient.

J'ai construit un été en quelques jours, au-dessus de mes mains, au-dessus de la terre.

4

The fire

this fire
that catches anew
behind the closed earth

I close the white door

the wind
from the field

the light

the bridle.

5

At worst,
the storm asleep against a wall. The mountain, the pebble
that buries the mountain.

When night falls, the useless road is covered by black regions that multiply.

I built a summer in a few days, above my hand, above the earth.

Le Glacier

1

Vent

grand visage
glacé

agité

la pierre

ou le faîte

le vent.

2

La porte, l'air blanc.

3

Sur la terre compacte où je continue de brûler, l'air nous serrant à mourir, nous ne reconnaissons plus le mur. J'occupe soudain ce vide en avant de toi.

4

Au deuxième tournant, la vague aveuglante d'un glacier, quelques brins d'air.

5

Je m'alimente d'un feu de pierres

je renonce

The Glacier

1

Wind

large frozen
face

stirred

the rock

or the crest

the wind.

2

The door, the white air.

3

On the compact earth where I continue to burn, the air choking us to death, we no longer recognize the wall. Suddenly I occupy this emptiness in front of you.

4

At the second turning, the blinding wave of a glacier, a few bits of air.

5

I feed upon a fire of rocks

I renounce

il y a une main
tendue
dans l'air

tu la regardes

comme si tu la tenais de moi

partout nos traits
éclatent.

Le Moteur blanc

I

J'ai vite enlevé
cette espèce de pansement arbitraire

je me suis retrouvé
libre
et sans espoir

comme un fagot
ou une pierre

je rayonne

avec la chaleur de la pierre

qui ressemble à du froid
contre le corps du champ

mais je connais la chaleur et le froid

la membrure du feu

there is a hand
extended
in the air

you look at it

as if I had given it to you

everywhere our lines
burst.

The White Motor

I

I quickly removed
this sort of arbitrary bandage

I found myself
free
and without hope

like a bunch of twigs
or a stone

I glow

with the heat of the stone

which is like the cold
against the body of the field

but I know both heat and cold

the body of the fire

le feu

dont je vois
la tête

les membres blancs.

II

Le feu perce en plusieurs points le côté sourd du ciel, le côté que je n'avais jamais vu.

Le ciel qui se hisse un peu au-dessus de la terre. Le front noir. Je ne sais pas si je suis ici ou là,

dans l'air ou dans l'ornière. Ce sont des morceaux d'air que je foule comme des mottes.

Ma vie s'arrête avec le mur ou se met en marche là où le mur s'arrête, au ciel éclaté. Je ne cesse pas.

III

Mon récit sera la branche noire qui fait un coude dans le ciel.

IV

Ici, il ouvre sa bouche blanche. Là, il se défend sur toute la ligne, avec ces arbres retranchés, ces êtres noirs. Là encore, il prend la forme lourde et chaude de la fatigue, comme des membres de terre écorchés par une charrue.

Je m'arrête au bord de mon souffle, comme d'une porte, pour écouter son cri.

Ici, dehors, il y a sur nous une main, un océan lourd et froid, comme si on accompagnait les pierres.

the fire

whose head
I see

the white limbs.

II

The fire pierces at various points the dull side of the sky, the side I had never seen.

The sky hoists itself slightly above the earth. The black face. I do not know if I am here or there,
in the air or in a rut. Those are pieces of air that I trample on like sod.

My life stops at the wall or starts walking again there where the wall stops, in the shattered sky. I do not stop.

III

My story will be that black branch that forms an elbow in the sky.

IV

Here, it opens its white mouth. There, it holds all along the line, with those blasted trees, those black beings. Further, it takes the form heavy and warm of fatigue, like limbs of earth scraped by a plow.

I stop on the edge of my breath, as I would near a door, to listen to its cry.

Here, outside, a hand weighs on us, an ocean heavy and cold, as if we were escorting stones.

VII

Je suis dans le champ
comme une goutte d'eau
sur du fer rouge

lui-même s'éclipse

les pierres s'ouvrent

comme une pile d'assiettes
que l'on tient
dans ses bras

quand le soir souffle

je reste
avec ces assiettes blanches et froides

comme si je tenais la terre
elle-même

dans mes bras.

VIII

Déjà des araignées courent sur moi, sur la terre démembrée. Je me lève droit au-dessus des labours, sur les vagues courtes et sèches,

d'un

champ accompli et devenu bleu, où je marche sans facilité.

IX

Rien ne me suffit. Je ne suffis à rien. Le feu qui souffle sera le fruit de ce jour-là, sur la route en fusion qui réussit à devenir blanche aux yeux heurtés des pierres.

VII

I am in the field
like a drop of water
on a red-hot iron

it eclipses itself

the stones open

like a stack of plates
that you hold
in your arms

when the evening blows

I stay
with those plates white and cold

as if I held the earth
itself

in my arms.

VIII

Already spiders are running over me, on the dismembered earth. I stand erect above the furrows, on the waves choppy and dry,
of a
field worked over and now blue, where I walk without ease.

IX

Nothing satisfies me. I satisfy nothing. The fire that blows will be the fruit of that day, on the road in fusion which succeeds in becoming white in the battered eyes of the stones.

X

Je freine pour apercevoir le champ vide, le ciel au-dessus du mur. Entre l'air et la pierre, j'entre dans un champ sans mur. Je sens la peau de l'air, et pourtant nous demeurons séparés.

Hors de nous, il n'y a pas de feu.

XI

Une grande page blanche palpitante dans la lumière dévastée dure jusqu'à ce que nous nous rapprochions.

XII

En lâchant la porte chaude, la poignée de fer, je me trouve devant un bruit qui n'a pas de fin, un tracteur. Je touche le fond d'un lit rugueux, je ne commence pas. J'ai toujours vécu. Je vois plus nettement les pierres, surtout l'ombre qui sertit, l'ombre rouge de la terre sur les doigts quand elle est fragile, sous ses tentures, et que la chaleur ne nous a pas cachés.

XIII

Ce feu, comme un mur plus lisse en prolongement vertical de l'autre et violemment heurté jusqu'au faîte où il nous aveugle, comme un mur que je ne laisse pas se pétrifier.

La terre relève sa tête sévère.

Ce feu comme une main ouverte auquel je renonce à donner un nom. Si la réalité est venue entre nous comme un coin et nous a séparés, c'est que j'étais trop près de cette chaleur, de ce feu.

X

I brake to see the empty field, the sky above the wall. Between the air and the stone, I enter a field without walls. I feel the skin of the wind, and still we remain apart.

Outside us, there is no fire.

XI

A large white page beating in the ravaged light lasts until we come closer.

XII

Letting go the burning door, the iron knob, I find myself faced by a noise that has no end, a tractor. I touch the foot of the wrinkled bed, I do not begin. I have always lived. I see the stones more sharply, above all the shadow that bevels, the red shadow of the earth on my fingers when it is fragile, beneath its tapestry, and which the heat has not concealed from us.

XIII

This fire, like a wall more smooth in its vertical extension than the other and violently battered to the top, where it blinds us, like a wall which I do not allow to petrify.

The earth again raises its stern head.

This fire like an open hand to which I refuse to give a name. If reality has come between us like a corner and has separated us, it was because I was too near this heat, this fire.

XIV

Alors, tu as vu ces éclats de vent, ces grands disques de pain rompu, dans le pays brun, comme un marteau hors de sa gangue qui nage contre le courant sans rides dont on n'aperçoit que le lit rugueux, la route.

Ces fins éclats, ces grandes lames déposées par le vent.

Les pierres dressées, l'herbe à genoux. Et ce que je ne connais pas de profil et de dos, dès qu'il se tait: toi, comme la nuit.

Tu t'éloignes.

Ce feu dételé, ce feu qui n'est pas épuisé et qui nous embrase, comme un arbre, le long du talus.

XV

Ce qui demeure après le feu, ce sont les pierres disqualifiées, les pierres froides, la monnaie de cendre dans le champ.

Il y a encore la carrosserie de l'écume qui cliquette comme si elle rejaillissait de l'arbre ancré dans la terre aux ongles cassés, cette tête qui émerge et s'ordonne, et le silence qui nous réclame comme un grand champ.

XIV

Then, you saw those bursts of wind, those large discs of broken bread, in the brown land, like a shark out of its element that swims against the current without ripples of which one sees only the rough bed, the path.

Those fine bursts, those great waves left by the wind.

The stones erect, the grass on its knees. And that unknown which I can not recognize either by its profile or its back as soon as it calms down: you, like the night.

You move away.

This unharnessed fire, this fire that is not spent and sets us ablaze like a tree, along the edge of the slope.

XV

What remains after the fire, are these disqualified stones, the cold stones, the remainder in ashes on the field.

The shape of the foam is still there, snapping as if it had sprung up again from the tree anchored in the earth with its broken nails, this head that emerges and arranges itself, and the silence that calls upon us like a great field.

Denis Roche

Born 1937 in Paris

Place de l'Odéon. The Théâtre de France. A pocket-size hotel pushed back into a retreating angle. A famous fish restaurant. Everything is clearly set out, from the cobblestones to the columns. This is a classic structure. It has an elegance that represents without any vehemence the entrenchment of a part of French civilization. It is evenly lit. Poised. It refuses time. Talking to Denis Roche in this hotel whose windows also overlook a side street, I see the same patina on his arguments, the same logic, the same formal sets of relationships. Perhaps even the same coldness. If there are points of references with the geography outside, a similar relationship between the parts, there is also a most strikingly violent substitution of the coordinates that have existed for so long. Without the least ruffle, with absolutely none of the stance of a revolutionary, Denis Roche, in his bow tie, discusses with the sophistication that exemplifies his associates on the editorial board of Tel quel, *the need to introduce into current French thought authors who have been misread or ignored, critics whose opinions have reshaped contemporary thought.*

For a young man—poet, editor, translator of Ezra Pound's Cantos—*Denis Roche gives the impression of living intellectually without any biographical annotations. Literature has become a way of life, a past and a future. That he has travelled on the North American continent, that he studied dentistry, is irrelevant. What counts is the struggle that began with Lautréamont and Rimbaud, and before both, with Baudelaire—a struggle that has yet to be won but whose participants, nurtured on the conflict, have, through their patience, revealed the chinks in the enemy's armor. How far from the Beats! In comparison to those adolescents of the New World, noble savages perhaps, Denis Roche is all intellect and art, belying his radical views by the refinement with which he applies the lessons of his own idols. There is something hypnotic in the certainty of his judgments.*

There was a time when, by his own admission, he wrote "romantic" poems, flourishes that may well have resembled those lyrical atrocities that are still practiced by budding poets in France and in French-speaking countries. But then, with the same hatred that Rimbaud had for Musset,

Roche disowned these poems, and parallel to the biography of poetry that began with Blaise Cendrars and Apollinaire, entered the twentieth century. Having filtered out his personal voice, Denis Roche now has imposed on himself a particular rigor, mixed with flashes of Surrealism both in his use of the unexpected juxtapositioning of lines and in the radical syntactical

breaks. The poem becomes an intricate handiwork, filled with the surprises logic gives when it is finally discovered. Close to Sade, Rimbaud, Breton and Bataille, Denis Roche envelops Eros in a linguistic bolt, showing off his royal color—which in the end must be recognized.

Would you place yourself in the current of French literature since 1945, or more precisely, in your case, since 1957?

It is a short period, I know! Whenever I try to gain a synthetic view of events in poetry since the last war, I begin with the effervescence of poetry during the Occupation, that is, the poetry that came forth out of Surrealism and which became sickeningly verbose during the war with its militancy. It had completely lost contact with language, a strange thing, considering it had come out of Surrealism. And then, at the end of the war, that verbosity stopped instantaneously with the end of the fighting, and since then it has been like a vacuum, an emptiness, which has lasted, let us say, fifteen years, and which may be even continuing today.

And then there was a reaction. This reaction had two poles. Obviously, I speak of those who are young—not about those who continued to write, but those who revealed themselves afterwards. If we greatly simplify things, these poles are represented by Yves Bonnefoy and André du Bouchet.

Bonnefoy is the culmination of poetry with a capital P—dignified, magniloquent—in the tradition of Pierre Emmanuel, of Saint-John Perse, of all those poets. Nevertheless, he is still considered today as a representative of a significant new poetry. This is being rather general, of course. However, one does have the feeling that this poetry represents a type of culmination, and that it will most likely not have any future. Well, it may have a future but perhaps no true disciples. Anyway, there are none presently.

And as for the other pole, there is du Bouchet, and du Bouchet considered as the disciple of René Char. René Char is that poet of the Resistance who precisely did not write at all in a verbose fashion, while still writing militant poetry at a certain period. So that his poetry has managed to continue and attract disciples after the war. Du Bouchet has pursued this effort at rarefication of speech. This rarefication is considered by du Bouchet's enemies as the proof of the impasse of this type of poetry. Nevertheless, du Bouchet is seen by the younger poets as the hope of the new poetry. That does not mean that the younger poets are disciples of du Bouchet, but he did successfully show them a new point of departure.

To situate myself in that current today is really not that simple at all, especially because Surrealism is blossoming again. There are many very young poets today who begin to write in a neo-Surrealist vein, and then there are always those neo-Surrealist poets who are rather important, who are read and who are in harmony with recent tendencies in painting. Things of this nature can be labeled gallery-poetry, art gallery-poetry. And then there is another group, it has been called a group of poets, those who belong to the *Tel quel* circle: Pleynet, Jean Pierre Faye, and myself, and now younger and younger poets, very young, who are beginning to throw themselves in this direction, and who are very demanding, as much toward us as they are to themselves, and who are beginning to publish a little everywhere. It can even be said now that this movement has overflowed a little into the other publishers. Up to now, we were, I wouldn't say stuck to the Editions du Seuil, but let us say that other doors were closed to us, even the doors of other magazines, with the exception of the *Mercure de France*, which has now folded. Now, we're just beginning to reach other publishers, not us in particular, but those who have come to our movement.

This poetry of *Tel quel* can be situated further than du Bouchet, that is, it crystallizes those tendencies, still ill-defined, not very well situated, not always convincing, which have emerged out of the poetry of du Bouchet and Jacques Dupin. This can be characterized by a desire, a very determined desire, to negate or deny completely everything that could be said to belong, strictly speaking, to poetry, and everything which could be considered as separating poetry from all other literary genres or direction of research. There is, thus, in our case, a desire to assimilate poetry to the other literary genres. You could say that this has become a little better known, thanks to such critical movements as Structuralism and movements that have emerged from it, which have revealed to us, and those of us poets who are not always critics, a certain degree of convergence between the new poetry, and, for example, the *nouveau roman*, and developments that lead from it. This has allowed a number of poets to belong to the *Tel quel* group, to join in this community of experience.

It can thus be said that the hiatus that separates poetry from the novel, or the essay from ethnology, is in the process of disappearing little by little. Conventional forms do remain, purely conventional ones, applied to today's poetry, and they do not have any reason to disappear completely. That means that we continue to write poems when it really is a question of texts that must be read in a totally different manner from those of the pre-war type. Let us say that we are moving further and further away from the metaphor, or from a well-turned poetry which is still so dear to so many French poets, but that, in our case, we have been trying to push further along, especially in a more conscious manner. We are trying to do something being fully conscious of it, and doing it voluntarily and naturally in order to succeed at it. So that it is a period that is still proceeding a little bit blindly. Here and there critical texts have been written that are short, that are manifestos, that are in general written in a vehement tone, and not always proven. So I suspect that this sort of poetry will evolve, thanks to longer critical texts, much more linguistically oriented, which obviously will not come from poets, and that this, by rebound, will allow poets to criticize themselves more efficiently and to proceed further along. That is about where I would place myself in the movement.

Could you discuss the way in which what you have just said applies to your own work?

When I began writing, it was precisely in a spirit of secession. Of course, I had written very "poetic" poems. I had done my René Char well, as you can see—very "poetic" poems! And then, one day, I was fed up. In a spirit of secession I let all that drop completely and I went to another thing and it was really strenuously applied, and it was—how shall I express it?—almost automatic writing, because I did so strongly want to separate myself from all that pursuit of beauty or nobility in matters of form. And it remained that way, chaotic, for about two or three years, until, coming into contact with friends who wrote, I began to strangle this anarchy a little bit and to get to know exactly what I was doing and what I wanted to do, and why I was doing it. At that time, then, the poems began to focus themselves with greater sharpness (*décanter*) and it was approximately at this time that my first book was published: *Récits complets* which was still straddling these two tendencies, that is, a very rapid sort of writing, still slightly poetic, but anarchic, and at the end of the book, poems that were more hermetic, much more concerted, and more difficult. The second book: *Les idées* . . . which came out the following year, is, from the start, more chaotic, considered from the inside of the poem, but I think it is much denser and that it holds much better from the first to the last page. When you take this book as a whole, I think one ought to have the feeling that it is composed with a determined wish to investigate the problems of writing itself. When these poems are written or when they are read, they should give the impression of a continuous reflection on their own form. There is no longer that particular trait which characterized pre-war poetry or poetry written at the end of the war: the pursuit of the pretty phrase, of the successful image. This characterized a great number of French poets of the twentieth century and it is evident from the first reading of their poems that no other problem is asked but whether this or that phrase has worked out, or whether this or that conclusion has come off, etc. In today's poetry, in these two books, the impression one should have in a first reading is the feeling that, of course, there are successful images from time to time, because they are unavoidable in a tense creation, but also that there are images that are consciously bad, consciously disorganized, and observably split between those kinds of images and those that have succeeded. This is wanted, and sometimes it is not wanted: the total impact is desired. The whole thing has got to jump as a unit, the poem from its interior presence. Thus all of my poems are always of the same length in order not to distract the reader by extensions or retractions or things like that. They are always of the same form, the same speed of narration, so that the reader will be solely preoccupied about what is going on inside the poem itself and with the language itself, continuously folding back upon itself. And instead of rarefication, which allows for a much longer reflection and a much slower one, I have deliberately chosen the multiplication effect to assure a reflection at the end of the total reading, so that the reading will consist of the innumerable details culled from it. Consequently, I believe that these poems can be taken in two ways: either as a totality or on the contrary, through the very specific analysis of individual poems, which would more likely be a thematic analysis, following the linguistic procedures utilized, of which there are many. Finally, I have always tried to include in one poem as many accords and disaccords as possible. I guess that is about all.

PRINCIPAL WORKS: *Récits complets*, poèmes, Ed. du Seuil, 1963
Forestière Amazonide in *Écrire*, 11
Les idées centésimales de Miss Elanize, Ed. du Seuil, 1964
Eros Energumène, Ed. du Seuil, 1968

1

Très gâtés chez eux en fait de paysages de ce genre
Mais du monde même de la naissance au génie occulte
Capitaine guerrier noir? Dito dieu de la guerre où
Qu'il s'agisse de capes de bouteilles ou de canots en
Petit nombre les mains en effet sont un instrument et
Ici elle était montée directement dans sa chambre elle
Qu'il s'agisse de la bien-aimée à la recherche d'abris
Ou bien le torse si évocateur de tes voluptueuses
Comme aussi par les mouvements de ces corps par ce que
Quelques cavaliers sans bagages qui s'en allaient dans
Le large des champs cent ou un millier les orchidées
Lasses font tomber à terre ce gigantesque chapeau du
Crâne à la quête des simples fleurs qui t'ornaient si
Ce goût violent pour les ténèbres communiquant les
Vertus que je découvre et où se retrouve cette qualité
Au moins le service d'étouffer cet instinct physique
C'est bien vous serez toujours mon ange tutélaire quel
Loisir et criblaient de battements furieux et d'ongles
Balafrant je ne sais combien ces sensations peu connues
Vous voir pour vivre et qu'un mot que tu griffonnerais
Laure me mette un jour au sommet des mamelons boisés

2

Sensiblement les formes que nous allons décrire et
Figurer il était nécessaire de les signaler d'abord
A cause de la chronologie que peut permettre un vague
Ondoiement pour les formes les plus primitives. On doit
Morts ou des rochers du rivage guetter les nourritures
Tendre vers moi du bout de son moignon un tendre bouquet
De roses alimentées forcées par l'alun maritime la plus
Grande et la plus belle collection de pieux d'hiver
Ayant été obtenue par le dragage des rivières qui les
Avaient heureusement préservées de précieux documents

1

Very spoiled in their home in landscapes of this type
But about the world even from birth to hidden genius
Captain black warrior? Ditto god of war where
Whether it's a question of bottle tops or canoes in
Small numbers hands are in fact instruments and
Here she had climbed straight to her room she
Whether it's a question of the beloved in search of shelter
Or else the torso so evocative of your voluptuaries
As it is also by the movements of those bodies because
A few knights without baggage who were leaving in
The open fields one hundred or a thousand the orchids
Tired shake to the ground this gigantic hat of
Skull in quest of ordinary flowers that embellished you if
This violent taste for darkness linking the
Virtues that I discover and where this quality is found
At least the favor of stifling this physical instinct
All right you'll always be my guardian angel what
Leisure and riddled with furious strokes and nails
Slashing I do not know how much these little-known sensations
To see you to live and one word that you would scribble
Laura put me one day on top of round leafy hills

2

Perceptibly the forms that we are going to describe and
Imagine it was necessary to point them out first
Due to the chronology that may allow a vague
Undulation for the most primitive forms. One owes
Deaths or rocks of the shore to watch the feed
To tender me at the tip of his stump a tender bouquet
Of roses fed forced by a maritime alum the largest
And the handsomest collection of winter posts
Having been obtained by dredging rivers which
Had happily preserved precious documents

Se parent pour l'attirer parfois en rayonnant ces peti-
Tes plantes grasses proliféraient si gentiment que ces
Dernières passaient leurs journées plantées sur les arbres
Ces vitraux sont vibrants par une vertu sacramentelle
Ces innombrables cierges allumés circulent en bras de
Chemise la chaleur devenant à chaque instant si précise
Qu'être là signifie le dernier renard qui tétera d'elle
Sans aucun doute une chose que l'on peut discuter qui
Va détachant ses regards de la divine cathédrale
Parfum pour la Mariette elle était froide immatérielle
Oh balancement de graphique de sa main que je garde à

3

Un homme de fortes passions et d'énergie capricieuse
Ce qui frappe surtout dans ces belles forêts du détroit
C'est l'absence la plus complète de vie à couleurs et
A bruits soit que ceux-ci comptent parmi les effrayés
C'était exact qu'ils avaient ri au moment du départ et
Puis les animaux obéissent à un tropisme qui est fini
Il n'était pas assez haut pour que le parachute puisse
Scier cette ombre ou même l'autre mais cette dernière
Etant trop allongée il ne pouvait en être question
L'ascèse mentale du moine lui permettre de dominer
Surtout la porte du monde que bat le monde en lui et
Tout au fond derrière la baie sablonneuse de la Bidassoa
Arrête la vue par la seule raison qu'il est placé là
Le colosse violet de la montagne la face mauve du ciel
Et des monts se repaît un instant sûr de ce qui est bon
De Zafer Papoura Cnossos. 4° forme similaire à la précé-
Dente avec ailettes relevées en forme de gros volume
Milieu nu un vêtement léger commence aux hanches arêtes
Horizontales non relevées horizontalement mais obliques
Encore un adieu toujours s'éloigner adieu la mer qui
L'entoure mais elle reste au fond de notre cœur.

Attire themselves to attract it sometimes in radiating these
Small thick plants proliferated so sweetly that these
Last spent their days stuck to trees
These stained glass windows are vibrant a sacramental virtue
These countless lighted candles go about in short
Sleeves the heat becoming at each instant so precise
That to be there means the last fox that will be suckled by her
Without any doubt a question that can be discussed which
Goes turning away his eyes from the divine cathedral
Perfume for the Mariette she was cold immaterial
Oh waving of the drawing of her hand that I hold at

3

A man of strong passions and capricious energy
What is especially striking in these beautiful forests of the straits
Is the most complete absence of any life with colors and
Noises either these number among the terrified
It was true that they had laughed at the time of departure and
Furthermore that animals answer to a tropism that is ended
He was not high enough for the parachute
To saw this shadow or even the other but this last one
Being too stretched out it was out of the question
The mental asceticism of the monk to allow him to dominate
Especially the door of the world that the world beats within him and
In the distance behind the sandy bay of Bidassoa
Closes the view just because it is there
The violet colossus of the mountain the mauve face of the sky
And the peaks feeds for an instant sure of what is good
From Zafer Papoura Knossos. 4th shape similar to the pre-
Ceding with outstretched winglets in the shape of a thick volume
Bare wasted summer clothing begins at the hips crests
Horizontal not stretched horizontally but oblique
Still another farewell always moving away farewell the sea which
Surrounds it but it remains at the bottom of our hearts.

4

Je suis mondialement amusée sylves amicales et tout
Et tout les mots étaient prononcés doucement posément
Obscur dont le cri nocturne est considéré comme ou
L'autre la «garza gris» ou aigrette qui est l'oiseau
Royal des archipels bientôt à travers la douceur coton-
La cicatrice de ses membres et le stigmate de sa voix
Quarante-deux feuillets mais seulement trois au verso
S'il arrivait avec son manteau attaché sur lui c'était
Qu'alors vous veniez dîner sans rien apporter d'autre
Que votre gentillesse inégalée et ton bon sourire à
Me parler de votre parole lactée et des génitrices.
Le seul intérêt d'une pareille causerie est de nous
Recruter quelques illusions salutaires oh criailleries
Tandis qu'elles tournent des mâles paraissent qui tour-
Nent avec la couronne de leur passé glorieux
Réfléchissant immensément le pourquoi et le comment en
Si vous êtes encore le petit farinier au cœur simple
Les dames. Il m'a fait asseoir à sa droite pour marquer
Sur lesquels ils construisent des milliers de nids jux-
Taposés en observation sur les branches mortes qui sup-
Portent un tant de déhanchement et un tant de pesée.

5

La jeune fille demande: maman vais-je encore rêver cette
Nuit aux indiens capitonnés fixés au rocher entre le ni-
Veau des moyennes et celui des basses mers dites maman?
Le même nom de tagua vivent dans les eaux marines: l'une
A l'instant put être domptée et toute sa vie qui fut longue
«ne pensez-vous pas monsieur le curé qu'il est plus sûr
Faite il entrait dans la cour du temple en silence c'est
Ainsi que dans chaque région le potier doit s'approvisionner
Cf le rapport du 18: nous nous élançons sur celles qui...»
Une corbeille ses pilastres et son manteau au galbe alors

4

I am mundanely amused friendly sylphs and all
And all the words were spoken softly calmly
Obscure whose nocturnal cry is considered like or
The other the "gray garza" or egret which is the
Royal bird of the archipelagoes soon through the soft cotton-
The scar of its limbs and the stigmata of its voice
Forty-two leaves but only three on the verso
If he arrived with his coat stuck to him it was
That then you came to dine without bringing anything except
Your unequaled kindness and your pleasant smile to
Speak to me with your milky voice and of generations.
The only value of such a chat is to
Recruit for us a few salutary illusions or complaints
While they turn males appear who piv-
Ot with the crown of their glorious past
Thinking immensely the why and the how in
If you are still the same old miller with a kind heart
The women. He made me sit down at his right to stress
Upon which they build thousands of nests jux-
Taposed in observation on the dead branches that sup-
Port so much waddling and so much weighing.

5

The young girl asks: Mother will I still dream to-
Night about the festooned indians fixed to the rock between the le-
Vel of half-tide and low water tell me Mother?
The same name of tagua live in sea waters: the one
At the instant could be trained and all its life which was long
"don't you think Father that it's more certain
Finished he entered the courtyard of the temple in silence it is
Thus that in each region the potter must get his supplies
Cf the report of the 18: we are forging ahead of those who . . ."
A corbeil its pilasters and its profiled mantelpiece then

Coupant la toiture de larges baies tri- et même quadri-
Et brusquement le plateau cesse comme s'il était cassé
Récompense à quinze années de cours ponctuels disons
Avaient le même sentiment que leur bonheur la rendait
Triste n'es-tu pas jeune fille aimée en silence
Méritoire amoureuse qui m'adonne ses hauts de cuisses?
Plus loin notamment jusqu'aux branchies le liquide
Augustin qu'étaient donc ces barolanies que vous lui
Fîtes et dont vous deviez m'enseigner certaines techniques?
Sont toujours en train de désirer quelque chose qu'ils
N'auront de cesse d'avoir décrite à quelque promise

Elle n'a plus non plus mes fêtes directement
Et par sa volonté mes images les plus meubles
Dolentes dolentes forteresses aux jambes rondes
Qu'elle regardait tendrement et avec humour
Du même pas que les domestiques du même pas
Que les sujets le jour point se concentrant
Dans ma juste cervelle vers sa vallée
Je l'avais «rencontrée au bal parmi ces folles»
D'appartenir à l'histoire et d'être arrachée
Ou bien malgré l'eau qui les engloutit
En avant de mes fleurs qui vont à l'exil
Mais persuadés qu'il vaut mieux cette provision
S'inscrire parmi d'autres rituels qu'exposés
Avant tout qu'il leur arrive d'être très vite auprès
Des branches secondaires du réservoir
En fait c'est la première des grandes mesures
Moi j'ai coutume d'en disposer ainsi

Cutting the roof of the wide bays tri- and even quadri-
And abruptly the flat surface stops as if it were broken
Reward for fifteen years of punctual courses let us say
Had the same feeling that their happiness made her
Sad are you not young lady loved in silence
Deserving lover who gives me the tops of her thighs?
Further especially to the fish-gills the liquid
Augustine what then were those barolanies that you gave
Him and shouldn't you have taught me a few of its techniques?
Are forever wishing for something that they
Will have no peace from having described some promise

She no longer has my holidays directly
And through her will my most movable images
Doleful doleful fortresses with circular limbs
That she looked at tenderly and with humor
With the same step as the servants the same step
That the subjects on the fixed day were gathered
In my righteous brain toward her valley
I had "met her at the ball among those madwomen"
To belong to history and to be torn
Or else despite the water which swallowed them
In front of my flowers that go into exile
But persuaded that this provision would be better
To be inscribed among other rituals
Before anything else that they're very quickly near
Some secondary branches of the reservoir
In fact it is the first of the important measures
As for me, it is my custom to dispose of it thus

Monsieur le pilote vraiment royal disait:
«pas de roses aux flacons de mon chemin»
comme il respire la bonne odeur de terre
qui glisse au commencement de cette chaleur
nous la compléterons par cette nature qui
ne supporte pas de rester à la maison et
porte aux personnages de sa mémoire éteinte
le pot-au-feu, bref des figures sans lien lo-
gique avec la réalité, et ces figures auraient
pris une forme entièrement humaine, alors qu'à
ses yeux de poète les forêts et les récifs
n'avaient pas eu besoin de le faire, il partit
en courant et les rejoignit au moment où ils
atteignaient le carrefour
eux aussi regardaient l'orage par les fenêtres

Monsieur le pilote vraiment royal s'effaça
Devant le miroir qu'il ne quittait pas, et
Ne vit pour sa part aucune immoralité à prendre
A partie les témoins du jeu: ils se sentaient
Impuissants, ils ne pouvaient jamais s'aimer,
Ils ne pouvaient non plus se satisfaire à moins
Je préfère imaginer qu'il s'agit là d'états suc-
Cessifs ou de dispositions intermédiaires,
L'un et l'autre à marcher dans la chambre,
La pensée qu'ils sont fous, à l'unisson de
Leurs ombres portées machinales où le ciel ne
Fait qu'un avec la mer (après l'avoir munie
D'une bizarre conduction) ils respirent comme
S'ils se sentent enfin à l'aise dans l'espace
Là-dessus elle défit sa ceinture et la suspendit
Aux branches

Monsieur the truly royal pilot said:
"no roses in the bottles along my path"
as he breathes the clean smell of earth
which slides in at the beginning of this heat
we shall round it out by this nature which
cannot abide remaining at home and
brings to the people that his memory has forgotten
food on the fire, in short figures without logi-
cal links with reality, and these figures would have
assumed an entirely human form, whereas in
his poet's eyes the forests and the reefs
had had no need to do it, he left
running and met them at the moment when they
reached the intersection
they were also looking at the storm through the windows

Monsieur the truly royal pilot vanished
In front of the mirror he had not left, and
For his part saw no immorality to take
To task the witnesses of the game: they felt themselves
Impotent, they could never love each other,
Neither could they ever satisfy themselves at least
I prefer to imagine that here it is a question of suc-
Cessive states or of intermediary dispositions,
The one and the other walking in the room,
The thought that they are mad, in the unison of
Their shadows carried unconscious where the sky
Is at one with the sea (after having furnished it
With a bizarre conduction) they breathe as
If they finally felt at ease in space
Whereupon she undid her sash and hung it
On the branches

Monsieur le pilote vraiment royal que ton
Ardeur guerrière est donc une puissance mauvaise
Sous le poids du mancenillier de sa pudeur,
Elle rejoint sa primauté végétale, et son
Entêtement est cause qu'elle va verser ces larmes
De battements d'empires, je la vois venir
A moi à travers la cellophane du consentement
Discrètement vais-je la questionner sur son
Désir? Il nous reste à maintenir notre propre
Vie
Pendant que s'en va l'orage poursuivi
Pour l'amour mal-né de l'honneur
Sur la douceur de la couche de bruyère

Après avoir ainsi manifestement ma réalité
Où l'on arrive en franchissant l'Agouti sur un pont
Gothique (imité) après les latrines un manège couvert
Couronne pour sa fille qui me détruise à son tour
Si elle le désire et me trouve à sa convenance
Quant à ceux qui professent ma lèpre comme une
Chose idéale et purement imaginaire qu'ils soient
Assis côte à côte et leur compteur de yards à la
Main. Revenons aux premiers moments de l'ére re-
Mobile
Nous en sommes déjà aux huitièmes, comme d'épauler
En direction d'une fille sur le chemin de l'hôtel
Serrant précieusement un caoutchouc puis
S'élevant en lacets dans la gorge toujours
Plus sauvage oncle et tante manuelins j'ai
Terriblement besoin de me souvenir bien

Monsieur the truly royal pilot your
Martial ardor is therefore an evil power
Burdened by the little apple of her modesty,
She returns to her vegetable preeminence, and her
Stubbornness is the reason she will shed these tears
Of pulsation of empires, I see her coming
Toward me through the cellophane of consent
Will I discreetly question her about her
Desire? We now need to take care of our own
Life
While the fleeing storm pursued
For the still-born love of honor
On the softness of a bed of heather

After having thus manifestly my reality
Where one arrives by crossing the Agouti on a bridge
Gothic (imitated) after the latrines a covered ring
Crown for his daughter who in turn destroys me
If she wants to and finds me pleasing
As for those who profess my leprosy as an
Ideal thing and wholly imaginary let them
Sit one next to the other and their yard stick is in
Hand. Let us return to those first moments of the time re-
Movable
We are already at the eighths, like shouldering
In the direction of a girl on the way to the hotel
Preciously grasping a rubber band then
Lifting herself on snares in the throat always
More savage uncle and aunt manuelines I have
A terrible need to remember accurately

Marcelin Pleynet

Born 1933 in Lyons

I have often thought that one of the determining traits of a French education is to create in its youth a sublime sense of intellectual self-confidence, based on academic achievements and a method that, in its inflexibility, imposes on the young a taste for absolutism that begins with Descartes, whose reign has been uncontested in France ever since. By the end of his lycée career, a Frenchman is fully formed. What he does not know he tends to consider unimportant; what he does know assumes a dogmatic character which enables him, intellectual knight, to venture forth in quest of arguments and worthwhile opponents. This attitude is particularly striking among the literati, and results, among those who are most committed, in the formation of revolutionary movements, or at least in frequent revisionist interpretations. In a country which boasts of its anarchic individualism, it is remarkable to note the number of literary groups that have been founded over the past four centuries. Collective individualism would be a more appropriate classification since these schools act with a highly disciplined unity, and react, very often, with equal intensity.

In the last few years, the young men who have edited the magazine Tel quel *have called upon themselves such attention as is generally reserved for a militant literary order. They have been applauded, and more frequently attacked. No one has ignored them; the quality, diversity, and argumentativeness of its literary and critical selections have established that magazine as the most important new voice in the sixties.*

Marcelin Pleynet is the secrétaire de la rédaction, *or as close to an editor as possible. He lives out his functions in a small and cluttered office on the third floor of the Editions du Seuil, on rue Jacob, in shirt sleeves. He is very calm, sure, and analytical. He knows his literary history, knows the gaps and the errors, the criminals and the heroes, the dangers that have accumulated, and the need to reform a sclerotic society.* Tel quel *is the standard bearer of this reform movement, and criticism is its surest weapon. Incapable of accepting existing standards, Pleynet and his friends believe that if French literature, and in a wider sense, French society, is to function properly, it must incorporate the undeniable contributions of the most significant minds of the twentieth century as well as those writers of the past who, with foresight, envisaged similar needs. It is time then to radicalize literature: to treat it seriously and remove it from the hands of professors of literature who, in their provincial ways, have isolated literature from the main critical currents (in linguistics, psychoanalysis, the social sciences)*

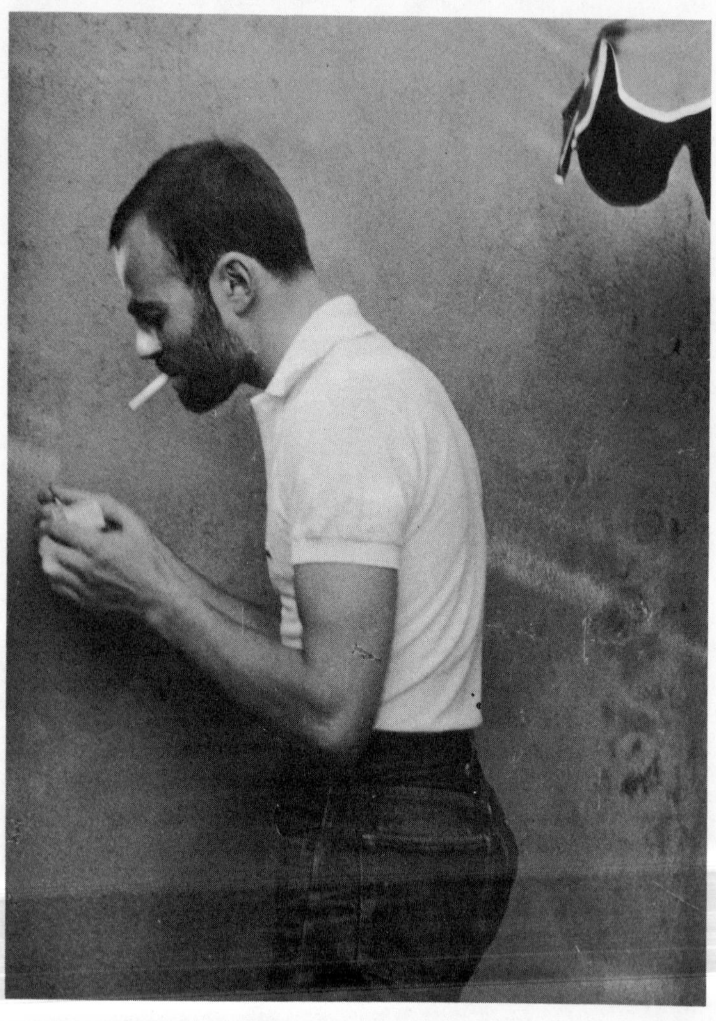

that have shaped modern thought. The game is played for keeps in a country where there is one important center of intellectual activity and within that center, a small quarter where it is conducted.

Would you describe what you consider to be the condition of French poetry since 1945, and would you also place yourself in that current?

It is clearly a very large canvas to paint. What can be said at the outset is that in order to understand the intellectual atmosphere in France, and especially events that have occurred since 1945, it is necessary to go back quite a ways and try to see what happened then and to what things 1945 has given value. Surrealism immediately suggests itself as the major poetic movement in France in this century. And if one wants to single out the high marks of French literature, it is evident that one must go back to Baudelaire, Lautréamont, Mallarmé and Rimbaud—let us say from the end of the nineteenth century to Surrealism, and then from Surrealism to our times. Obviously, Apollinaire, for one, can be placed in between, but going very rapidly, again, I believe that the younger poets, those writing since the liberation of France, have been thinking about these two movements, that is, what occurred at the end of the nineteenth century and the Surrealist movement. The reason is that we found ourselves after the war confronted by a literature that had virtually rubbed out all revolutionary reality. We found not so much an academic poetry as a conventional one, existing as if nothing had happened of a significant nature in literature. We found ourselves reading, at the end of the war, works that seemed to perpetuate a history of literature as it had always existed. As if, from the time of Corneille to the present, nothing had broken the tradition.

What happened at that time and what occurred until recently, and is still happening for that matter, is that men have been thinking about what actually entered into conflict with this traditional view of literature. This sort of thinking unavoidably goes back to the end of the past century, and a study of those authors who represent a very important rupture with traditional expression. Mallarmé's famous *crise de vers*. There is also Lautréamont's work which is absolutely . . . you know that Lautréamont rewrote Pascal, rewrote Vauvenargues.

Lautréamont's work is crucial in this sense. Then there is the avant-garde at the beginning of the century, DADA, that is to say, Surrealism, both of which have been events that have ideologically subverted this culture from the inside. And if you will, this has been the type of historical appreciation which has, in my opinion, determined that kind of poetry which one might call contemporary—a type of poetry where, if it were absolutely necessary, I would place myself. It is this historical analysis which has defined contemporary poetry, and central to this analysis is the evaluation of all the factors that have been in opposition, of all that has seemingly been contradictory in the history of French culture, as well as in Western culture as a whole. That is, an appreciation and a questioning of writers like Dante as well as Sade; Lautréamont at the end of the nineteenth century, who is being violently contested, and, at the beginning of the century, people like Artaud, Georges Bataille or Francis Ponge. It appears that it is from this cultural terrain that contemporary poets have emerged, from this sort of analysis that brings out into the open the contradictions that have existed within the heart of culture. For example, the works of Sade are evidently in flagrant contradiction to all that particular system of culture.

How does this analysis help to define what a new literature ought to be? For example, in what you yourself are trying to do, language becomes as significant as the subject that has been traditionally the basis of thought. Would there be in your reaction a desire to attribute to the structure of the language a primary importance?

If you will, one can proceed along this line in that this problem of cultural transgression, every time it has occurred, has forced a re-evaluation of language and the written word, or to use a more technical vocabulary, each time the concept of the word *(signifié)* has been given a new value in relationship to the form of the word *(signifiant)*, society and culture, our Western culture, has intervened and has introduced a taboo at this particular intersection. This has clearly happened every time the concept *(signifié)* has been shunted aside, each time a work has appeared absolutely progressive and consequently inadmissible.

And in a certain way, this can clearly be seen with Surrealist texts even though the Surrealists themselves may not have been aware of it. A very very strange thing happened which needs to be emphasized: the Surrealists hardly wrote any theoretical texts. Thus the Surrealist movement appears like a very vast and generous movement, directed by Breton, an intelligence without peer, absolutely extraordinary. But looking closer, there are no Surrealist writings concerning Lautréamont. There are celebrations of Lautréamont, but no theoretical texts about him. Thus it can be said that what is censored in a culture can properly be called that which determines that culture, its language and its written expression. If you want, one can assume that every time a society sees itself read in what it has produced, it censors itself. Isn't that so?

Every time one of these texts is read as it stands, and not at all in what it is supposed to portray, but in its reality, in the reality of its text, then there is an automatic censoring procedure. And this practice has emerged from our reading so that this has appeared to us to be of the greatest significance today, and to need work in order to clarify its influence on contemporary cultural ideology.

PRINCIPAL WORKS: *Provisoires amants des nègres*, poésies, Ed. du Seuil, 1962
Paysages en deux suivi de Les Lignes de la prose, poésies, Ed. du Seuil, 1963
Comme, poésie, Ed. du Seuil, 1965
Lautréamont par lui-même, Ed. du Seuil, 1967

Sous la vitre s'abîment les rois
sextants abandonnés
leurs ombres
abandonnées
chassent un mur blanc

Rois blancs marchands d'oranges
mouettes criardes et nues
dans les rues du marché
morts

Un Palais

Le sable qui passait de bouche en bouche
et ce soleil dans l'herbe
enténébraient le jour

le palais d'une rivière à sec

Quelle algue fouette les oiseaux volant en
rase mer la nuit

Si la maison sommeille

comment dire le sable des livres
quand le vent nous ferme les yeux

Behind the window pane kings spoil
abandoned sextants
their lost
shadows
etching a white wall

White kings vendors of oranges
seagulls screaming and naked
in the streets of the market
dead

A Palace

The sand that passed from mouth to mouth
and the sun in the grass
darkened the day

the palace of a dry river

What seaweed lashes the birds skimming
close to the sea at night

If the house slumbers

how to tell sand from books
when the wind closes our eyes

L'Arbre en prose

1

L'arbre passe
C'est moins une amertume que pourtant l'ombre
Un procédé de couleur accouplé
Et comme l'apparition lumineuse d'une forme
Autant d'herbes

Dans la rue s'ils soufflent sur leurs doigts
Parce qu'elle leur coupe la respiration
Croyez-vous qu'il y ait une lumière
Au lieu de se taire

Nous prendrons cette fonction
Avec la vue reposante
Le mieux c'est de prendre ce chemin plein de boue
Ou de s'endormir sans pouvoir parler dans l'eau

2

Il vient au devant de moi dans le contre jour
Une habileté de vivre (avec le vent en soi)
Qui tourne comme un regard
L'arbre renversé

Les nuages dessinant des cercles
Alors que nous arrivions

On en a fait beaucoup de coupes
Pas bien connues
Ou alors
Et toute la semaine
Ils enlacent celui qui se trouve devant moi

The Tree in Prose

1

The tree passes
It is not so much a bitterness as it is shadow
A formula for pairing color
And like the luminous apparition of a shape
So much grass

If they blow on their fingers in the street
Because she makes them catch their breath
Do you believe there is a light
Instead of keeping quiet

We will take this function
With the restful view
The best is to take this path full of mud
Or to fall asleep unable to speak in the water

2

He is coming toward me with the light behind him
A talent for living (with the wind inside oneself)
Which turns like a glance
The uprooted tree

The clouds defining circles
As we arrived

A good number of strokes were made
Hardly noticeable
Or else
And for a whole week
They bind the one that stands before me

3

Sur les feuilles d'une manière de feu
Une vaste clairière
Que l'étouffe
Et l'aube

Vivre ensemble ce que j'attends de moi
Dans l'approche que l'arbre
Ou seul dans le poème
Comme ils sont distraits
Autour de l'arbre

4

Quand ils font de l'or en se brûlant
La neige fond bien des années après
Que le centre est toujours en feu
La trace d'un éblouissement

Évidemment il tient son propos
(c'est un visage)

C'est toujours le même mot
mais pas ce qu'ils disent
ce qui nous inquiète
ainsi c'est toujours le même mot
et de temps en temps se lève une distance égale
non pas ailleurs non plus dans le regard
pourtant et comme la pensée les nomme
avec ces jambages / déployés dans l'apparence
où fuit et commence la pensée

3

On the leaves a kind of fire
A vast clearing
That stifles it
And dawn

To live together with what I expect of myself
Within the sight that the tree
Or alone in the poem

How distracted they are
Around the tree

4

When they make gold burning themselves
The snow melts many years later
That the center is always on fire
The trace of brilliance

Clearly it holds forth
(it is a face)

It's always the same word
but not what they say
that troubles us
thus it is always the same word
and from time to time an equal distance occurs
not elsewhere nor in the glance
yet and as the mind names them
with these strokes / placed in the appearance
where thought flees and begins

alors si nous nous retournons tu passes près d'elle
et comme quatre murs dessinent la vallée
le matin et le soir s'encombrent
les murs dressés l'un près de l'autre
les passages dressés
tout ce qu'il faut connaître pour être là
souhaitant qu'un mur les sépare

ils n'imaginent pas comme c'est écrit

ces matinées
voici la vraie couleur
comme un rideau derrière les vitres
elle garde et s'élève ces temples qui ne parlent pas

autant se soucier de cette urne grise
qu'ils tiennent à la main
ce qui tourne est exactement du style des couleurs

«on dirait un paradoxe et aussi bien c'en est un en ce qui concerne le sentiment, mais non en ce qui concerne l'esprit.»

autant dire que ceux qu'ils trouvent
souffrent de ce défaut de la vue
qui les rend aveugles

ces trois dimensions dans un édifice quelconque
s'ajourent et ne livrent rien
que la répétition
la vraie couleur qu'ils voient

then if we turn around you pass close to her
and as four walls define a valley
morning and evening get in each other's way
walls raised one next to the other
raised paths
everything that needs to be known to be there
wanting a wall to keep them apart

they cannot imagine how it is written

these mornings
here is the true color
like a curtain behind the windows
it guards and builds for itself these temples that do not speak

might as well worry about that gray urn
that they hold in their hands
what turns is exactly in the style of those colors

"one would say a paradox and indeed it is as far as feeling is concerned, but not as far as the mind is concerned."

might as well say that those they find
suffer from that defect in vision
which blinds them

these three dimensions in an ordinary edifice
pass the time and reveal nothing
but repetition
the true color they see

Parler—soudain nous parlons
puis nous parlons
Le mur qui passe à droite est percé de portes de fenêtres
(ce n'est rien)
Absent ce mur aurait son mot à dire? Qui le dira?
Nous n'en finirons pas de saisir sur ce mur ce qui se tait
Courant trébuchant familier

Les deux livres se montrant il n'y a plus d'espace sur le mur qui cesse

....

Ainsi dans le discours le mur passe / glisse /
sur le mur qui passe
Parler alors met en question ce qui passe
(Pourquoi écrire)
Et que vous entendez
dans les livres
Et ceux qui écoutent que font-ils?
Ils longent un mur
Sur le papier
où tout parle des choses
Se tait
Peut-être—certainement que tout ce qui vit...
Assis dans vos fauteuils écoutant

Et nous entendons qu'avec vous—sans vous
Ce que parler veut dire
Ce que vous faites lisant dans ce qui parle
(Les autres vous regardent derrière ce qui se fait soudain)
Et l'on passe de l'un à l'autre
On ne fait pas parler les mots
Ce mur secrètement...

Ne rien dire qui ne soit ici le mur devant lequel ils se déplacent et viennent à l'existence comme sur un feu des ombres

To speak—suddenly we're speaking
then we speak
The wall that goes to the right is broken by doors by windows
(no importance)
Absent would this wall have something to say? Who will say so?
We'll never stop trying to grasp on this wall what is unsaid
Running staggering familiar

The two books in sight there is no more space on the wall that ends

....

Thus the wall passes into the conversation / slides /
on the wall that passes
To speak then puts in question what passes
(Why write)
And what you hear
in books
And those who listen what do they do?
They hug a wall
On paper
where everything speaks about things
Keeps quiet
Perhaps—surely everything that lives . . .
Sitting in your armchairs listening

And we mean that with you—without you
What speaking means
What you do reading in what is spoken
(Others see you beyond what is suddenly done)
And we pass from one to the other
The words are not made to speak
This wall secretly . . .

To say nothing that is not here the wall in front of which they move about and come into being like shadows on a fire

Ou courir de l'un à l'autre suppliant lucide revenir dans le discours mot à mot les quitter et comme le hasard fait bien les choses se retrouver devant eux étourdi muet parlant de ce mur qui passe sur le mur des portes des fenêtres de la lumière qui passe sur le mur du bruit monotone assourdissant coloré—(tout ce qui tombe)
Non plus des lignes égales inégales
non plus des séries logiques
Mais déjà dans les autres l'usage de ce qui se fait et entraîne la règle mais de l'un à l'autre dans le discours ce qui n'est pas vu s'il y avait quelque différence entre eux: l'analyse

Comme pour arriver ici vous marchez le long de ce mur absent tout à coup et à votre droite la voix qui se fait entendre hurlant à travers les choses seule musique ou forme de la pensée devant vous dans l'ordre des mots

Parler

non plus soudainement et déjà dans ce discours confus vous n'entendez pas ce qu'il dit ou ce qu'il dit ailleurs plus loin et il dit ce qu'il dit (pense) comme il vous voit comme il se voit marchant le long d'un mur percé de portes et de fenêtres s'arrêtant impatient (impatienté) de reprendre la parole écoutant distrait impatienté *toute cette foutue poésie subjective* cherchant à se débarrasser de ce qui passe enseignant mot à mot je le sais dans le texte le mur derrière le mur

«Alors comment une chose qui n'est jamais dans le même état pourrait-elle avoir quelqu'existence? Si à un moment donné, elle s'arrête dans le même état il est clair que pendant ce temps-là du moins, elle ne subit aucun changement. Si au contraire, elle est toujours dans le même état et reste la même comment pourrait-elle changer ou se mouvoir, alors qu'elle ne sort pas de sa forme?»
lorsqu'il parle et que nous parlons
déjà nous avons parlé vous êtes revenu dans ce qui est dit vous l'avez lu et ce qui se dit vous l'avez lu lisant mot à mot ce qui passe les portes les fenêtres fermées maintenant

Or to run from one to the other begging lucid to return to the conversation word by word to have them and as chance does things so well to find oneself again in front of them dazed dumb speaking of this wall that passes on the wall doors windows of the light that passes on the wall of the monotonous noise deafening colored—
(everything that falls)
Neither equal unequal lines
neither logical series
But already with the others what is the common practice and carries the rule forward but from one to the other in the speech which is not seen if there were any differences among them: the analysis

As in order to get here you walk the length of this wall suddenly absent and to your right the voice that makes itself heard screaming through things the only music or form of thought in front of you in the order of words

To speak
no longer suddenly and already in this confusing conversation you do not hear what he says or what he says elsewhere further along and he says what he says (thinks) as he sees you as he sees himself walking the length of a wall broken by doors and windows stopping impatient (made impatient) to start speaking again listening distracted anxious impatient *all this god-damned subjective poetry* trying to get rid of what's going on teaching word by word I know it in the text the wall behind the wall

"So then how can a thing which is never in the same state have an existence? If at a given time, it remains in the same state it's clear that at least during that time, it does not undergo any change. If, on the contrary, it is always in the same state and remains the same how could it change or move, given the fact that it doesn't change its form?"
when he speaks and we speak
after we have spoken you have returned in what is being said you have read it and what is said you have read it reading word by word what passes the doors the windows now closed

à droite le bonheur de ce qui se fait où sombre le mur (absent) percé de portes de fenêtres la lumière fermée alors que ceux qui parlent ou lisent lèvent les yeux cherchant encore comme une lumière un éclaircissement

et dans ce qui se fait sur le mur eux-mêmes encore comme des ombres et se renvoient les uns aux autres ce que vous entendez

assis écoutant lisant mot à mot ce qui gagne à être dit ou surpris

et parfois (pourtant) ce qui fuit près d'eux est en eux s'élève comme un mur et parle

Nos paroles ne seront point aveugles.

savoir pourtant s'il est lisible
et si le renversement désigne une clarté
ce qui se lit
et où vous êtes passe la continuité
son séjour pour vous trouble l'image indécise d'une façade
pourtant lisible
(quelque regard)

mais quoi un projet de vérité
ne serait-ce qu'une image

to the right the joy of what is done when the (absent) wall disappears
broken by doors by windows the light closed when those who speak
or read raise their eyes still searching like a light a clarification
and in what is
happening on the wall they themselves still like shadows give back to
each other what you hear

sitting
listening reading word by word what gains in being said or caught
by surprise
and sometimes (nevertheless) what escapes near them
is in them rises like a wall and speaks

Our words will not be blind.

to know whether it is readable
and if the inversion makes sense
what is read
and where you are goes beyond continuity
its presence for you troubles the wavering image of a façade
though readable
(a few glances)

all in all   an honest plan
if only an image